The Anxious Lover

Overcome Anxiety, Manage Conflicts and Improve
Your Relationship

Nora Williams

UP

URANUS
PUBLISHING

Uranus Publishing

Contents

INTRODUCTION

Do you have doubts that you're not with the "proper" spouse –
that you're "settling" and that there's someone "better" out
there for you?

Do you fear that you don't love your spouse enough, that you're
not "in love," that you're not "attracted," or that something is
"missing"?

If you answered yes to even one of these questions, this book was written for you.

Anxiety can be entirely debilitating for the individual that suffers from it. It can make it difficult to function in school, work, social interactions, and more. When you are anxious, you are constantly in survival mode, acting as though your death or demise is imminent. It is something that comes on suddenly when you least expect it to and can cause a myriad of problems for you. You can be entirely fine one minute and then suddenly shift over to a full-blown panic attack the next minute. People around you may feel as though you are losing your mind, or you may be convinced that you have something seriously wrong with you.

Anxiety is the most common mental health disorder that you can have. It is estimated that upwards of 285,000,000 people worldwide suffer from some sort of anxiety disorder, and it may be easy to understand why surviving is hard. It is tough to live in a world that largely does not care about you when you understand that that is the case.

We can define what it is and identify several different kinds of anxiety disorders that people can suffer from. We understand how to treat the symptoms and make sure that those who suffer no longer have to.

Frequently, certain markers make someone more or less predisposed to developing anxiety in the first place and foremost, women tend to develop anxiety disorders more frequently than men for currently unknown reasons. A family history of people having anxiety can also indicate increased risk, such as having a parent, grandparent, or sibling that has suffered from anxiety in any form. Major trauma can also cause an increased rate of anxiety if you have lost a loved one unexpectedly, such as a child or spouse. If you have been the victim of some sort of traumatic event like an assault, you are more likely to develop anxiety at some point. Changes to your life, such as divorcing unexpectedly or having children, can also bring about anxiety, particularly right around when it has happened. Lifestyles can also impact the risk of anxiety, with those who smoke or consume caffeine in excessive amounts being at an elevated risk. Lastly, those who endured abuse or trauma in childhood are also likely to show higher anxiety results.

If you are reading this book because you suffer from anxiety, you may have an anxiety disorder. However, you don't need to have a diagnosed anxiety disorder for anxiety to negatively affect your life. The distinction is a matter of degree: the extent to which your anxiety interferes with your full functioning and enjoyment of life, including your enjoyment of your relationship. Common to all expressions of chronic anxiety is a pervasive sense of fear and uneasiness that interferes with feeling that you are okay.

Chapter One

WHAT'S MAKING YOU ANXIOUS?

Anxiety can make you feel trapped and think that no one understands what you're going through. It's a horrible monster that enjoys dragging you down and placing your mind in solitary confinement.

When you find yourself feeling alone, I want you to close your eyes, take a deep breath, and imagine yourself in a peaceful place full of love. Imagine the warmth of the sun as it feels like arms wrapping you up in a hug. Imagine the smell of your favorite flower. You can imagine your family, friends, and anyone else with you smiling as they too feel the warmth and smell the flowers. Hold this image for a few seconds to help you remember you're not alone.

Understanding Anxiety

You know that you have anxiety, and it probably affects various parts of your life. For example, you feel anxious at work, driving in bad weather, meeting a new person, or in your relationship. But have you ever honestly looked at what anxiety means? Anxiety is your body's natural response to stressful situations, such as public speaking, starting a new job, getting married, or taking a test. This means that, to an extent, it's normal to have anxiety during specific situations.

At this point, you might be asking why anxiety doesn't feel natural. If it's normal to have anxiety during stressful situations, why does it make you feel like something is wrong or not doing something right? For instance, you start dating someone who you think is the one. You met them a few weeks ago and talked on the phone daily, but you're getting ready for your next date and feel nauseous. You keep rubbing your palms on the towel because they're sweaty and focus on deep breaths when you feel your heart racing. If anxiety is normal for your body, why are the symptoms hard to handle?

First, it's because you don't truly understand how to control anxiety and what's happening to your body. You don't know where your anxiety stems from or what strategies to help you through a stressful situation. Second, your brain isn't wired for you to feel happy. It's wired for your survival. This is why people tend to feel anxiety or like "something bad will happen" when they're happy. For example, you survived negative emotions such as shame and fear throughout your childhood, so now your body and mind follow this script. Therefore, when you're happy and feel your life is going well, your mind kicks your anxiety into high gear.

Feeling relationship anxiety is normal, no matter what stage your relationship is in. Not only can it happen when you start dating, but anytime down the road when you're facing a negative event or facing an uncertain future. For example, if you're laid off from your job, you'll start to experience anxiety in your relationship. You and your significant other might start arguing more, especially about finances. You might even question if you're with the right person because you're starting to look at their spending habits in more detail. Plus, stress makes you feel unhappy, and this emotion can creep its way into your relationship, causing both you and your partner to feel unhappy in the relationship.

These might be words your mother told you when something bad happened, and you didn't know how to handle it. It's true, and one of the best pieces of advice I can give to my clients—the anxiety and all the emotions with it will pass. The situation that's causing the anxiety will pass. Furthermore, the stress won't cause a profound and long-lasting effect on your relationship. Stress is temporary, and one of the best steps you can take is to let it affect you temporarily and then move on.

External Causes of Relationship Anxiety

External causes of anxiety are normal to have in a relationship. They'll last from the time you start dating until the end of your relationship. External causes focus on the forces that aren't in your control, such as work, living arrangements, extended family, or your partner.

It's normal for you to feel more anxiety in your relationship during the beginning because you don't know the person well enough to start letting your guard down yet. This may even be the case when you feel like you're in love with your partner and you begin to wonder if they're the one. You might even dream about marrying them one day and still feel high anxiety. This happens because our hearts tend to work a little faster than our brains. In other words, your brain continues to make you feel anxious while your heart is falling in love. Once your brain catches up with your heart, your anxiety will drop. However, this doesn't mean that you'll never feel anxiety again throughout your relationship. It'll always come and go, depending on several factors.

One of the biggest reasons for anxiety is money, even when bills are paid and you can spend money on items you don't need. For example, you have enough money to put a down payment on a new vehicle, trailer, or boat. Yet, you still feel that you never have enough money, or you worry about how you'll pay all your loans if you lose your job. Another way anxiety can rear its ugly head is through differences in spending habits. You might strive to save money while your significant other wants to spend it. You want to support them, but you also want to focus on your financial future. You want security when it comes to retirement and emergencies as they're bound to happen.

Another way finances can cause problems is living situations. For example, you're thinking of moving in together, but your partner wants a bigger apartment than what you feel is necessary. You might want to rent an apartment, but perhaps your significant other wants to buy a house instead. There are countless ways finances can contribute to anxiety in relationships, so you must bear these things in mind when making financial decisions in a relationship.

Body language is another type of language that can cause anxiety. For example, if your partner talks too widely with their hands or mimics your movements, you can feel uncomfortable, which increases your anxiety.

You're on a date with your partner when you notice they're smiling and waving to someone. They come up to your table, and your partner introduces them as a coworker. You watch as your partner continues to not only talk to them, but place their hand on their shoulder, joke with them, winks, and show other signs of frivolous behavior. Your anxiety starts to spike as you wonder how close friends and coworkers they really are because you don't act toward your coworkers in the same manner. Because of your anxiety, you'll start to pay more attention to how your partner reacts with other people. You'll start to notice every touch and sign of flirting, which will continue to increase your anxiety.

Another big reason for anxiety at the beginning of the relationship is a lack of trust. This is usually a temporary issue as once you start to get to know your partner more, and you'll start to trust them. When this happens, a lot of the anxiety you feel at the beginning will start to disappear. A few months into your relationship, your trust should be growing stronger. If it's not, you need to reevaluate your relationship.

Stress is a word in life that you can't fully escape. It doesn't matter if you have thousands of dollars in the bank, a great job, and a stable relationship—there will always be stress. Your anxiety will always spike when you feel stressed because it's a normal stress response. When you're stressed, you're worried about the future, or you fear what will happen. You have a feeling of uneasiness that you can't shake, and these factors lead you into anxiety territory.

Another common external cause of relationship anxiety is family. In general, any family member can cause a little more stress which leads to anxiety. Some of the family members, such as your children and parents, will have a major influence on your life and therefore cause you to feel more anxious in your relationship from time to time. For example, your children are sick, children aren't doing well in school, or one of your parents needs to go into the nursing home. These are normal factors that bring tension into your relationship, but other family members can become a central part that isn't normal. For instance, one of your siblings needs a place to stay because they lost a job, or one of your close cousins doesn't like your significant other.

Internal causes of relationship anxiety

Even if you've found the love of your life, you'll still have anxiety. Unfortunately, there is no cure for relationship anxiety because there are always external causes that you can't control. However, you should always be aware of the second type of anxiety—internal causes, which you can control. Unlike external causes, the anxiety you feel from internal causes will cause so much strain on your relationship that you'll find it crumbling around you. You could find someone you could never imagine living without, but your anxiety doesn't allow you to have a stronghold on the relationship. Just like external causes, there are several internal causes.

Past trauma and abuse are some of the biggest reasons for internal causes. For example, you recently left an abusive relationship and found yourself worrying that your new partner will start abusing you in the same way. You fear what'll happen during your first disagreement. Your past abuse might stem from your childhood, so when your partner becomes angry, it reminds you of being slammed against the wall or pushed down, and you fear your partner will perform the same action. Even if you've been dating for years, you can still find yourself struggling with past abuse and trauma.

Just like past trauma can cause anxiety in your relationship, so can past relationship failures. You've probably had a relationship in the past that you thought was going to last for the rest of your life but soon found yourself alone. You and your partner might have gone separate ways physically or emotionally. Either way, it's hard to find yourself alone, and learning to trust yourself or get out in the dating scene again isn't easy, especially if it's been a while. You might find yourself questioning what you can do differently now so you can ensure that this relationship lasts.

It's important to note that past trauma or relationship failures can cause another internal issue—fear of abandonment or worrying that your partner will leave you. No one wants to feel like they'll live alone the rest of their life, so when you've felt this before, you worry about it happening again. Fear of abandonment can strike if you felt alone most of your life, especially in your childhood. It can also happen if one or both of your parents left you and never returned. But, a fear of abandonment can happen without any past trauma or relationship failures. Psychologically, you need human interaction. You need to become attached to someone because your brain is wired this way. Therefore, when you feel that someone might leave, you become worried, and your anxiety spikes.

Fear also increases your anxiety by worrying that you'll get hurt or lose something that feels good. You want to feel that you're not only wanted but needed by your partner. You want to feel the love and passion that they have for you. Yet, you're anxious about these feelings because you can lose them, and this will result in you getting hurt.

Another way that fear interrupts your peaceful nature and causes anxiety is through rejection. You don't want to feel that someone doesn't want to spend time with you or doesn't like you enough.

Even if you're not sure that you want to become intimate with the person yet, you still fear rejection, which causes you to protect yourself in many ways. You might find yourself backing away from a relationship that's getting serious because of the anxiety you feel. You might also find yourself doing everything for your partner and pushing your needs and wants aside. You believe if you focus all of your attention on what your partner needs and wants, they won't reject you.

The attention you place on your partner can turn into another internal struggle known as jealousy. While a little jealousy in your relationship is normal and healthy, it can easily spiral out of control. When you mix jealousy with lack of trust and self-esteem, it becomes one of the biggest struggles in relationship anxiety. Think of it this way—when you're jealous, you fear the worst.

For example, your partner says they're going out to the bar with their friend, but you imagine them meeting another person and cheating on you. When they come home late, you start questioning them and accuse them of cheating. Soon, your argument is out of control, and you're losing sight of the love that your partner still has for you. Jealousy can also cloud the love that you have for your partner.

Finally, another big internal cause of relationship anxiety and one reason that often attaches itself to other causes is low self-esteem. When you have low self-esteem, it's hard for you to believe that anyone will treat you well. You expect the worst from people, and you believe that you deserve the worst. You might even find yourself questioning how someone could truly love you. You might start to believe that your partner is using you for their personal needs and will "toss you to the side" when they have what they want. There are a lot of negative thoughts that associate themselves with low self-esteem, and this creates anxiety.

What Questions Should You Be Asking Yourself?

Now, before you move on to addressing relationship anxiety, it's time to reflect and ask yourself a series of questions. The questions you ask yourself will depend on your experiences and causes of relationship anxiety (or what you believe to be your causes). You can start with a series of general questions that everyone should ask themselves and then move on to the personal questions.

When you come to this point, reflection is necessary. You've learned a variety of causes, but not all of them will resonate with you. You need to focus on the causes that you feel are a part of your puzzle. Ask yourself why you feel a certain cause is a part of your life and look at ways that you feel you can start to overcome them.

But first, take a step back from your reflection and start with some of these general questions, as they'll help lead you into your personal questions.

You need to ask yourself, "Do I see something developing from my relationship in the long run?" This is an important question to ask at the beginning of the relationship before you devote too much time to making it work. Like most people, you're more likely to become attached to the person when you put energy and time into the relationship. The more energy you give your partner, the harder it is to leave them. Reflect on your relationship now and think about your future. Do you see your partner supporting you in your dreams? Do they want to see you succeed? Do you see yourself marrying your partner and growing old with them?

Next, you should ask yourself, "Is my relationship worth working on?" It's important to ask yourself this question more than once as most people feel like they have the best relationship in the world at the beginning—meaning your answer is yes. But once you're a couple of months into the relationship, you might give yourself a different answer.

When you consider if it's worth working on your relationship, you need to look at several factors. First, you need to think about your goals and how they fit into your partner's vision and the relationship in general. For instance, if you notice your partner doesn't support your goals, it's time to look at how your relationship will affect your path in life and if this is something you want to change. You also need to decide if the change is worth it.

A third question to ask is, "Do I feel anxious because of my partner's actions or my fears or baggage?" Sometimes it's hard to determine the underlying cause of anxiety, and you need to take some time to reflect. However, you can usually gain an idea of what is making you anxious by thinking about the situation that happened before you started to feel your anxiety.

For example, you're having a discussion with your partner when it starts to become heated, and you feel it turning into an argument. Immediately, you start to feel your anxiety rise, so you back away from your partner and tell them that you need some space. You fear where the argument can go, so you feel you should have some time alone. While you're alone, you start to reflect on how a friendly discussion turned into a heated argument and why you became anxious. You think about your partner's past actions during an argument and realize there's no reason to feel fear. Your mind then takes you back to your childhood when you saw your parents arguing. You remember your father yelling at your mom, who just sat quietly at the table. You even remember when your father slammed his fist on the table a couple of times, which made your mother jump.

By reflecting on your anxiety, you learn that it stems from the past and emotional baggage you carry from your childhood.

After your reflection, you'll find your weaknesses that lead to your anxiety. Once you do, it's time to ask yourself, "Am I willing to address my weaknesses and work through my fears for my relationship?" You need to admit to your weaknesses and learn to overcome them because ignoring them won't help you or your relationship. In a sense, you need to ask yourself if you're willing to work on yourself for your partner.

It's not easy to focus on your weaknesses, and you'll find yourself struggling for several reasons. You might even find yourself sad or sinking into a depression as you start working on strengthening your weaknesses. However, once you make it to the other side, you'll feel like a new person. This doesn't mean you won't have weaknesses as they are a part of life. But, by working on them, you're working on a better life for yourself, your partner, and your future family.

In any relationship, you need to be happy with yourself. If you're not happy, then your relationship will struggle. Sometimes, becoming happy means changing your mindset, such as turning your negative thoughts into positive ones. Other times it means that you need to change your career path or make another life-changing decision. Even if you don't feel that your relationship is worth the change, let go of focusing on your relationship and focus on you.

It's important not to just look at your partner when you're analyzing your relationship, but you can't just look at yourself either. Always remember, there are two people when it comes to making a relationship work, and you both need to put forth the effort, or your relationship will become lost in the shuffle.

Chapter Two

SEX AVOIDANCE AND ANXIETY DISORDERS

I have no problem. I am not in the mood for such, and I think you should respect that and get your hands off me." Melissa told Brown in the heat of the moment. In their third year of marriage, Melissa and Brown are couples, and if there was anything Brown enjoyed in the marriage was their intimacy. Brown always looked forward to the next time they would lie in bed and make love to each other until they both reached the clouds. It was still a beautiful moment for both Melissa and Brown.

On the other hand, Melissa knew how much her husband loved her body never ceased to serve him some doses of her seductive body. However, the tables turned recently, Brown knew his wife had a problem, but he could not place his fingers on it.

Whenever he tried to initial intimacy, she always pulled back. The other night she was responsive, Brown had thought he had his foot on the door, but it was just a lie. As usual, Melissa was dressed in a short red gown; Brown could not resist what he saw, so he approached her, whispered in her ears the words she loved the most, and just there, she allowed him to have his hands plowing her body. Melissa was turned on in no moment, both lovers panting greatly, confessing how much they love each other and moaning simultaneously.

"Stop. I need to go." At first, those words sounded like a joke to Brown. Who says she needs to go away when she is horny and needs to be in the arms of her lovely husband. Confused, Brown turned over to the other side of his bed as he pondered on why his wife had been avoiding his touch for two months already. And the day she finally allows his touch, she needs to go. You could tell that Brown was angry, overwhelmed, but scared that his wife was sick or losing it. Melissa was always screaming his name in bed; he saw the look on her face, she desired him just the same way he desired to kiss her passionately that moment, but she needed to go.

One of the effects that anxiety is that it can alter your sexual life. In this story, Melissa was suffering from a particular disease, or problem and she is yet to talk to her husband about it. The same way you are interested in knowing the solution to Melissa's problem is how Brown was ready to look for the answer to her question. After considering certain options, Brown decided to visit a doctor specializing in sexual health.

"Your wife is healthy, and you should not think she is seeing someone else because she has been avoiding sex. It could just mean that she is nervous and anxious." The doctor said.

"But, we have been married for about three years now, and she had never treated me like a plague, even when she was traumatized by her brother's death, we still had sex a few weeks later," Brown said.

"There you go, Mr. Brown. Your statement just showed that your wife has anxiety history; what if she is having a recurrent, and she does not want to inform you, so she does not overwhelm you?" The doctor grinned at Brown.

The doctors would not have made more sense to Brown. He understood what the doctor meant and wondered if Melissa was really having a recurrent anxiety disorder or intentionally avoiding him.

I know Melissa can never avoid me like the plague.

What is sex avoidance?

Sexual avoidance can be referred to as avoiding sex or sexual moments literarily, and this only happens when an individual has been consistently having sex. In a more specific term, sex avoidance is a defense mechanism that people engage in. It could happen due to emotional distress, physical illness, panic attacks, and traumatic situations. It could also be an effect of impaired body image and low self-esteem. Sex avoidance can occur in any form; it could happen when an individual is addicted to sex or when the individual is experiencing some emotional surge. It could also mean that the victim may find it difficult to initiate sex with their partners. The America Psychological Association has classified sexual problems related to emotional issues as sexual aversion disorder. Because of this sexual aversion disorder, people avoid sexual contact with their partners. Amid an intense emotional surge, these people can kiss their partners passionately, but it becomes difficult for them to have sex with their partner because of genital contact. In complex situations, people with sex avoidance may avoid kisses and hugs.

Reasons for sex avoidance

What leads to sex avoidance? There are different reasons people can avoid sex, and one of the major reasons may be because the individual suffered sexual abuse as a child. For instance, Melissa suffered sexual abuse and harassment by boys in high school. She was an obese lady, and many boys harassed her by touching her body parts. The events continued for four years in high school, and during her prom night, her crush manipulated her to have sex with it. However, making love to Melissa wouldn't break her heart, but he recorded all sexual moments and sent them to other school students. It was a tough time for Melissa, and she attempted suicide three times. As a result of this, Melissa avoided sex until she got married. Brown was aware of her past; hence he tried his best to make her feel loved, cared for, and comfortable around him, but he wondered what he did differently to her that led to this.

On another note, not everyone who suffered sexual abuse as a child will avoid sex; some get sexually addicted. According to Mayo Clinic, below are the symptoms that people with an anxiety disorder may experience:

• Sweating

- Heart palpitations

- Irritable bowel syndrome

- Headaches

- Fatigue

- Insomnia

- Nausea

- Sweating

- Muscles tension, and aches

- Twitching

Why would the above symptoms cause people to avoid their partner?

Because sexual intimacy increases heavier breathing, it raises your heart rate and causes you to sweat. These symptoms are the same symptoms of the sexual aversion disorder, and these symptoms mimic the physical and typical "fight or flight" reactions. As a result of these reactions, many people tend to avoid feeling such again. Moreover, individuals suffering from anxiety disorders may avoid sexual intimacy to avoid events that trigger their memories and fears. According to studies, sexual activities can interfere with your emotions and can trigger worries about your body image, shame, and guilt.

Treatment of sex avoidance

The treatment of sex avoidance is dependent on the cause of sex avoidance, and treatment can either be a part of anxiety disorder therapy or therapy on its own.

• Sexual function can be improved with some medications, but most of these medications have different side effects. And one of the side effects is that it can delay orgasm and lead to premature ejaculation in men.

• For individuals who are already on anxiety disorder medications, ensure that you discuss with your doctor to adjust your medication to interact with the medicine.

• Cognitive-behavioral therapy can reduce fear, anxiety, and negative emotions. Cognitive therapy and psychodynamic therapy are usually conducted one-on-one and sometimes in a group counseling session.

I know you are wondering what happened to Melissa. Brown got back home after visiting the doctor and asked Melissa a few questions.

"Is there something you need to talk to me about? I mean, you have been avoiding sex? Are you hurt? Do you have flashbacks when we make love?" Brown asked Melissa all of those questions without hesitation.

"I am fine." She said, trembling and shaking.

"You are shaking. Should I take you to the hospital?" brown asked her, but she remained silent.

He cuddled her, and she felt relaxed almost immediately. Melissa looked into Brown's eyes; she could see the desire and hunger in his heart. She felt the same way, it had been two months, and she had tried to get out of the series of symptoms she experiences whenever she is about to make love to her husband. She moved closer to Brown and kissed his lips at first. Brown was surprised, but he remained calm and cool.

"I am sorry. I don't know what happened to me. I am sorry." Melissa said and continued kissing him, this time passionately. She whispered some dirty words into his ears, and the action began. After the lovemaking session, Melissa stated that she had been feeding her mind on many rape survivors' stories, and she had a conversation with a high school girl who was also a rape survivor.

Hence, the discussions brought back a series of memories to her; each time she remembered these people's stories, she experienced flashbacks. In the end, Brown was glad he got his wife back before it was too late, and both lovers got better and stronger.

Sexual avoidance can be cured; however, it can recur. So, anxious individuals must avoid activities that trigger anxiety disorder.

Chapter Three

COMMUNICATION IN RELATIONSHIPS

An intimate relationship is a close bond between two parties, in which they share their feelings, thoughts or spend their life together in any activity that reinforces the tie. However, relationships can never be obtained to certain individuals from distress, including unpleasant emotions, such as stress, frustration, and fear, after being attached for a certain time. It is undeniably normal for such marital disputes to arrive in the later stage of a relationship. Conflicts are frequently caused by an argument or unhappiness between the two parties. Consequently, this situation within the relationship will result in insecurity that will ultimately lead to a negative outcome.

The vital elements of the relationship are trust and mutual understanding. Without the existence of trust and understanding within a relationship, it is hard to believe that there has been no argument between both parties irrespectively of how deeply in love they are. On any occasion of fear, one party can often feel paranoid that the other party is unfaithful to their or not interested.

If this situation prolongs, it will aggravate the level of anxiety and possibly lead to the creation of negative intuitions in one's mind. If you encounter this, then you should take the first step to reconcile the lack of confidence in your relationship with your partner. Seek to resolve your current fear by respectfully disclosing your feelings of mistrust to your partner and digging down to the root causes of feeling worried. It is strongly recommended that all parties interact frankly to recognize and understand the root causes of this distress relationship.

Spending time together or taking part in any joint activities will also help to strengthen the tie. Going together for a vacation, for example. Having to enjoy the moment together at a wonderful place will allow both parties to recover the unforgettable memory while staying away from the stressful urban life at the same time.

In the relationship, one also needs to learn to forgive, accept, and negotiate. Controversy over an issue or so will not be beneficial to both parties. This will only cause more frustration or fear, which will inevitably deteriorate. Do not indulge in any inappropriate acts or words that may injure your loved ones. Furthermore, try to step back a little by tolerating him/her, just for a simple reason that you like about him/her as if when you first met, it brings you to the wonderful feeling. If you could do this way, the anxiety in your relationship would eventually cease.

Appreciation is another important factor in handling one another's frustration and fear about ourselves. Often making a rash decision, or moving too fast into a conclusion, won't help you find the answer. Anxiety at the onset of a horrific incident may be frightening. Why don't you learn to relax and be relieved by taking a deep breath and refreshing your memory on the things you both used to do together? Think of how amazing the ultimate bond that has brought you both together. Intimate greetings and body gestures will also help you show your partner that you care about them and help you express your feelings more implicitly. Having been through the process, you will realize one day that each of you will begin to respect each other naturally, even without the intervention of any 'mechanism.'

Moreover, good communication is one of the most valuable lessons we will all know in life. For a successful marriage, it is essential and goes hand in hand with a good one. This is the secret to maintaining a happy marriage. Good communication means that, when you communicate, you both understand each other. The faster you know how to communicate with your partner, the better the marriage. Why? For what? Since communication issues are the key reasons, or root cause, of the top issues that could divorce, split, or breed dysfunctional relationships among married couples.

Communication is important to everything you do in your marriage and with your partner. You and your spouse's desire and willingness are required to enhance communication within your marriage. An intentional effort will be expected from you and your partner to interact better in your marriage. By learning how to interact effectively with your partner, you can thrive in your marriage, do things you never thought possible, and excel in various areas of your life.

Importance of communication

People also ask which part of a relationship is the most important. Does it have compatibility? Have the same faith or political views in common? How about integrity, integrity, never struggle? Yes, the conversation is the key; contact, and as long as you can communicate and accept one another's views, you have a good relationship.

Yeah, what are certain issues to avoid while trying to interact with your partner? Okay, the way they communicate about their partner is a common mistake. You really don't want to be lectured unless you take a college class. Okay, the same way is your friend. Therefore, if you have an issue with any part of your friendship, do not sit with them and either read or yell at them. Communication is a bidirectional route. Talk to them, then hear them.

Honesty comes next. If your partner is worried about something or something in the relationship, you need to focus on saying so. Nothing hurts worse than a few people who keep it inside and let it rot. This would just poison the emotions and aggravate the friendship. This can be very complicated, indeed. When your wife disagrees, and you just want her, that will lead to a breakup.

Nonetheless, you are much better off than living together, and both finish miserable. But, on the other hand, you can find that they express your opinions when thinking about it, so the topic is readily appropriate. Finally, there is the consensus option. Perhaps you can't handle it exactly. Yet you should be able to find common ground because you are still fully committed to the partnership.

A very common error is that people don't even want to talk about it. We try to think about a big problem and then get side-tracked. That also occurs when one of you raises things to contend with that is difficult for the other; you are trying to change the topic to protect yourself. Don't make it as tenting as it might be. Keep your mind on the issue.

It is said that these days our lives are full. Work, families, interests, etc., fill our time and make a quick chat almost online by instant messaging! It can lead to another typical error for a couple: to either interrupt a discussion or attempt to do so in the turmoil of their lives. Speaking means just doing that! So, you all find a quiet and convenient spot to do that and avoid distractions. Even just before bed, don't wait until the last minute to try to have a serious conversation. Now is the time to talk about a romantic dream, not to buy a new car!

It may seem crazy, but you also have to date your friend. We are doing so much these days, why not a time to talk? And it doesn't have to be a deeply complicated problem. Anything is as easy as agreeing that you both go to breakfast every Sunday morning. Let there be a good local meal, a report on Sunday, and some anonymity. You eat, speak, listen, and then think about something that really matters. A partnership is like everything else in this world; it must be nurtured, nurtured, and nurtured if it is to become healthy, survive, and grow.

Verbal communication between couples

Verbal communication is the easiest and most commonly used form of communication. Words are easy to use to a large extent, and people like to hear things, especially when they are nice.

For instance, every spouse loves to be complemented through words 'you look very nice today,' 'I love you.' You are a great person with a fantastic personality.' Effective communication requires one to be able to express their feelings to their spouse through words. If a couple loves each other so much yet they are unable to communicate the same through words, they might never know how much they mean to each other.

Even when the actions show clearly that the spouses love one another, they still need to say it in words. Words will add value to the actions and vice versa. They will make the involved parties feel appreciated, loved, and sure about how the other person feels.

Along with all the compliments and expressions of the positive, the spouses can express what they are not happy about through words. If a spouse is doing something that is offending the other, yet the offended person is silent about it, the offender will most probably continue with their habits.

Silence does not help in most cases. If anything, a lack of communication will keep hurting the couple. One cannot possibly go through life while holding all the dissatisfaction inside. Verbal communication will help one let it all out.

However, when letting matters out, one should be discreet and careful. Care and warmth in communication are essential, especially when talking about matters that might bring disagreements. Couples should not wait too long before they say something about things bothering them. They should also not wait too long before telling each other that they care.

Nonverbal communication between couples

At some point in life, we have said something unpleasant or unfriendly to someone else. They might not have retaliated verbally, but they show their displeasure through facial expressions and actions, either voluntarily or involuntarily. The offended person did not have to say a word to tell the story, but it all showed on their faces. Human beings share more with their faces and body than they would give credit.

Spouses should be aware of their facial expressions and body language while talking to their partners to avoid giving off the wrong message. Human beings are capable of reading the body language of their partners, even subconsciously. If, for example, a couple is having a serious conversation and one person is hunched over and probably closed off, the other will detect a lack of vulnerability. Use the right facial and body language for every conversation.

For example, suppose a couple s having a serious conversation. In that case, the two parties must face each other and keep their body language open without crossing their legs or arms. The body language should show that the person is listening keenly, taking note of the important things, and is willing to work through the subject matter. Nonverbal cues are many, and they communicate to the partner either positively or negatively, even without an exchange of words. Everyone should be conscious and thoughtful of how their body language brings out their thoughts.

Communication issues in relationships

You already know that men and women don't speak the same tongue. In order to make a partnership succeed in the long term, it is necessary to learn how to connect well. That is to say, and when it comes to conversation, you must go on the same page.

As if it wasn't enough, some very prevalent contact issues also exist in marriages that can lead to instability if not recognized as the root cause of problems that can also ruin marriage in the end.

Let's take a brief look at four big relationship contact issues.

1. Before you speak, the partner anticipates your answer. This issue also arises in long-term relations. It is a kind of non-listening condition that tends to occur because you are not willing to listen to your friend. It's not just a one-sided deal. Often both of them start speaking over each other, while the

person speaking in other cases does not request a response. You will aim to establish successful two-way discussions by thought from the perspective of each individual. It will help minimize trust issues in relationships.

2. Thanks to our chaotic schedules in our lives, we do not seem to have enough time to share with our friends. Most conversation depends on conflicts, and there is little time to get back together and address more constructive topics. Most of the feedback is negative. Why not recycle, redistribute, and reorganize the requisite activities and spend one hour each day learning about more meaningful topics.

3. A dishonest party sometimes found in marriages is using deceptive trips to get there. If your wife criticizes you for any unnecessary transaction, for example, and you respond by reminding him of a mistake made in the past, you are trying to blame your wife. It is not a positive and beneficial approach. Do not give in to the pressure when the situation happens and stop the journey of remorse.

4. Somewhat like the guilt trip we just spoke about is now a mistake. A managing partner handles typically it. We blame our partner for everything so that we feel resentful and suffer from a lack of confidence and bad mood. If this form of conversation is the standard, it's time to speak seriously.

When you find all of these contact issues in your relationship, you will try to resolve them. The good things are that they can be patched. However, you want to make sure it is a joint effort. Operating with strong listening skills will improve friendship and performance well. In the end, you both would be much more comfortable and will be able to tolerate the ups and downs you face in life easier.

Communication mistakes and how to avoid them

We spend plenty of time reading and studying rules and more guidelines about how to make an effective conversation, but never do we hear people telling us these are the most important communication mistakes or how to avoid them.

If the connection is to occur with our children, our wife, friends, and colleagues, or with anyone with whom we get in touch for one or more purposes, we would have provided the details you are about to read to support us in a very significant part of our lives.

In most situations, we are advised that we will be transparent and precise as part of the negotiation process. That is, of course, entirely factual. We are trained to carefully examine our argument, stressing mostly the facts or material to see if the knowledge is right or not. Now, the origins of this knowledge are infinite for anyone who wants to use them. Everything can still be heard or discovered on whatever subject we want through books and magazines, radio, TV, newspapers, and the internet.

We already have the premise, the knowledge, and, with any luck, the opportunity to chat; that would be all we need, right? Okay, maybe not. We listed specificity and clarification to communicate correctly, which means that we should not necessarily use all sorts of meaningless terms or terms that do not actually mean something. This is very popular in the research and environment in which others seek to pretend to know everything. If we had to evaluate and quantify just how much time we expend to slip into the activity above, we would genuinely be shocked and attempt and eradicate instantly. It is much more realistic, straightforward, and rational and merely picks the words required to express our thoughts than letting a person pound his/her head trying to grasp half what we have spoken. We should encourage the poets to envision thousands of ways, for instance, to say, "I love you."

The above can be categorized in the contact cycle as content, but it is not everything. We lack anything that is so much forgotten: the type or theme we use. We are used to the hideous practice of using the most inappropriate means of voicing what we think, from frequent derogatory words or unnecessary tones to gestures that definitely say a great deal about the individual's education to the person receiving the details.

A few days ago, a nurse told me she was trying to fix the school assignment of her daughter by yelling at her: 'This is rubbish, you can't grasp this, and the teacher thinks you are crazy,' etc. Couldn't she even ask her, "Honey, is that the best you can do? I think you can do it well." Which of the two posts is likely to have a more positive effect on the student? While she had good intentions, neither the material nor the manner used by the mother to connect suggested that she was making an effort for her daughter at that moment.

The age, ability, and educational level of the receiver end and the moment and emotional state of the person listening to us are essential for adequate contact. While we use all of the above parameters to express what we desire, it does not guarantee that we are heard as we wish. We have the most outstanding radio or TV transmitter in the country and a decent system, but if radios or TV sets aren't on, our signal doesn't touch them, so it's pointless to check for other reasons.

Evidently, in each particular case, we should intensify and even consider the form of relationship between the people, the essence of the individuals we want to deliver our message to, and so on, to avoid the "no contact" that causes so many problems for those who still maintain that they call themselves moral.

Chapter Four

IDENTIFYING AND RESOLVING THE ISSUES IN RELATIONSHIPS

If you know what issues may arise in your relationship in advance, you'll have a much better chance to get past them. Although every partnership has its highs and lows, successful couples have learned how to handle the challenges and keep their love life going. They look forward to solving problems and learning how to navigate through complicated daily issues.

Many do so by reading books and articles on self-help, attending lectures, going to therapy, watching other successful couples, or using trial and error. In this part, we will explore those issues and problems that disturb your love life, and after identifying them, we will look into solutions for making a strong bond with your partner.

Problems arising in different phases of a relationship

When you get serious about someone, there are many things you need to know about them—in part to determine compatibility and in position, because communication, honesty, and confidence are the pillars of a healthy relationship. Often couples avoid these subjects or keep something secret that they think their new partner would not like.

The significant gaps that you end up noticing between you two should not be deal-breakers. And it does demonstrate that you know how to have a good relationship. And even the best pieces of advice on relationships can tell you the same thing. Now, let's look at which issues can arise in different phases of a relationship:

In the relationship's attraction phase, the brain actively releases dopamine and oxytocin while you are excited. It is this that contributes to euphoria and attachment feelings. Unfortunately, this hormone development amount does not remain for the relationship's lifetime since any person's brain has a defensive mechanism that needs protection perception.

As we go through different phases of a relationship, the feeling of security will be undermined at times. At this first phase of a relationship, the most common mistake is the inability to stick to your boundaries. Later it is to protect your principles, your morality, and your beliefs. You start to lose self-esteem. Upon reaching the following phase of the relationship, resistant circumstances will occur, such as when the partner who is not careful about eating also buys fast food for sharing.

In the dating phase of a couple's relationship, many people seek to turn their partners into perfect people because of the desires established from past failed relationships. That is why, at this point, a lot of couples split up and never go to the next phase. The truth is that, inevitably, many partners are lazy in their attempts to connect. They avoid focusing on their partner's good qualities and start concentrating that focus on their undesirable traits. It can lead to continuing resistance, feelings, and complaints, which usually is the major cause of a break-up in relationships.

Tension and tempers will rise at this relationship stage as both parties battle to be noticed and respected.

What seems to be a minor problem for one person can quickly escalate and be misunderstood by the other when it has not been communicated or understood. It also results in allegations of guilt and false charges.

In the disappointment phase, there is dullness as the relationship becomes secure. There is a lack of excitement and boredom at this point when some people start cheating in the relationship. In the stability phase, the biggest issue might be financial problems. It is possibly the top taboo subject in a relationship. We begin by being friendly, and then time brings up the money subject. A lot of couples, therefore, avoid thinking about money beforehand. It is why financial conflict always occurs at stage four after a couple has already moved in together. At this point, some couples even get married and then are unable to discover that they are having a financial dispute.

Constant arguments then undermine a sense of security, weakening the relationship's trust and protection. In effect, this makes you feel lonely and alone. Breakups are typically triggered by the related harm that happens when people's emotions are out of control.

In the commitment phase of a relationship, you can predict each other's decisions and actions; your partner seems predictable and boring. Your relationship may have been stagnant and lacks a romantic atmosphere too. People start taking their partners for granted. They cannot take good care of their appearance any longer or rarely put in the extra effort. There is no regard for the other person's needs, and real mutual interest seems to have fallen apart. That can make the partnership feel redundant.

Effective ways to resolve relationship issues

Relationships are complicated, but they don't have to be. Much of the time, regardless of their negative feelings and attitudes, the people make them complicated. Many of the issues arise because people are not very familiar with these different stages of relationships.

The more consciousness we have, the easier it will be to restore a relationship as problems arise. Concentrate on more reliable contact. If you feel, and it feels like you're not going anywhere, you're in the work stage. Plan the next as a pair of targets.

Essentially, the trick to going forward is to be mindful of where you are as a person. If you consider your relationship in the Coming Apart process, you don't have to give up hope. You can still bounce back into the phase of getting together. It takes effort and commitment from both sides of the parties, but you can revive a relationship that seems to be moving toward disaster. Some partnerships, however, cannot be repaired and should be set aside. It is up to both of you to decide where to pursue the happiness you both deserve—with or without each other. Let's find out how to do it:

Attraction phase

The first step of a relationship is to set your partner's boundaries to have reasonable expectations about their partnership with you. No matter how connected you feel early in a relationship, it's vital to communicate how you live your life and preferences honestly. Let the other person see that you have no pretenses. Maintaining your uniqueness is critical, as this is what initially generates attraction. Be clear about your limits, and try to make wise decisions where possible.

Dating phase

Respect your differences, and concentrate on being the best version of yourself to keep your attraction safe. And, in the long run, you will keep your partnership sustainable. Controlling your emotions and influencing your partner in the right way to build and sustain a happy and stable relationship is crucial. If your partner doesn't understand you or repeatedly appears to make the same mistake, try to help them instead of thinking they're not trustworthy and seek to undermine your relationship! Deal with your emotions as they get activated to ensure that your contact remains free, genuine, and transparent. It is the best way to understand each other and know what you can strive towards in the long run. A relationship can be a lot of work, but it won't feel like hard work if you both want to communicate effectively. It involves upholding the principles and ways of doing things and working as a team together.

Disappointment phase

To hold the peace at this level, you have to reintroduce novelty into the relationship. You can travel together, for example, and create new experiences that you share with your partner. Shared interactions are the foundation of a strong emotional connection.

Growing together is the secret to a lasting, healthy relationship. For example, attending workshops on personal growth, reading books, and even starting a business together. You both evolve in the same direction in this way, with lots of fun things to do together. However, maintaining the interests that fulfill each of you as an individual is also essential. It provides you with a natural break to want each other again and ensures fresh conversation material.

Stability phase

Have an honest conversation about money with your partner, and make sure you understand each other's principles and responsibilities in this respect. Perhaps one person wants to save a significant percentage of their income while others want to enjoy and spend a lot. That could become an issue in the relationship without a healthy discussion. A couple should then talk freely about their desires and find a compromise that works for both partners. A possible alternative is to provide a crystal-clear financial plan that is instantly implementable.

Commitment phase

The secret to a long-term, happy relationship is to carry back the courtship. Start to inspire one another with your efforts to bring your relationship back to life.

Offer each other gifts and, in the day, write or email a positive letter. Tell your partner how beautiful they are—passionately kissing each other every morning and night. Look with interest and uncontrollable desire in your partner's eyes, much as when your eyes first meet theirs. Practice this daily, and you will rekindle your early attraction and love one for another.

Chapter Five

HOW TO HELP YOUR PARTNER

Relationships and love demand that we get involved in our partner's life, which means we always have to be supportive and loving. If you have a partner with one or more types of anxiety, you are already aware of how it can influence your life and your life. You should know how to recognize the signs and learn how to neutralize an anxiety attack by relying on previous experience.

Your involvement in your partner's journey of learning how to live a life free of anxiety is of great importance. When it comes to sudden panic attacks, you can do several different things to help distract your partner and ease any suffering. When it comes to chronic anxiety, you are the one who will get involved in exposure therapy. There are specific strategies you can take into consideration when it comes to each type of anxiety.

This part will help you recognize which kind of stress your partner is struggling with and learn how to help him. You will improve and enhance your relationships' quality, strengthen the bond you have, and confirm your love and devotion to your partner.

Acute anxiety

Acute anxiety happens out of the blue. It can be caused by different things, specific situations, or other people you and your partner meet. It occurs suddenly, and there is no time for planning and taking it slow. You need to be able to react at the moment and to know how to assess the situation. Understand what is happening, what your partner is going through, and come up with the right way to neutralize the anxiety. There are four ways you can take to be supportive and helpful in case of acute anxiety:

Be calm, be compassionate. If you are not, you won't support your partner's needs at that moment. If you give in to anger, frustration, or anxiety, it won't help. It can even make things worse. You also need to remember not to give in to your partner's anxiety and accommodate it. In the long run, this is not helpful. Instead, offer understanding, not just solutions.

Assess your partner's anxiety. What level is it? What are the symptoms and signs of an anxiety attack? An anxiety attack can hit with a different strength each time. You need to recognize it to choose actions appropriate to the given situation.

Remind your partner of the techniques that helped with previous anxiety attacks. Whether it is breathing or exercise, your partner is probably aware of their success in neutralizing anxiety. But in the given situation, maybe they need reminding. Once they are on the right path to dealing with anxiety, your job is to provide positive reinforcement. Give praise and be empathetic once your partner executes techniques that will help with an anxiety attack.

Evaluate the situation. Is your partner's anxiety attack passing? If it is, be supportive and encourage your partner to continue whatever he is doing to lower his anxiety. If it stays at the same level or increases, you should start the steps from the beginning and develop different techniques and strategies to help your partner with an acute anxiety attack.

Chronic anxiety

To address chronic anxiety, you might have to try out exposure therapy, as it is considered the golden standard of treatment by many people. Usually, it takes the guidance of a professional therapist to try exposure therapy. But, if your partner's anxiety level is not severe, you might feel comfortable enough to try it on your own. In this case, you have to guide and learn how to support your partner.

Exposure therapy works by creating situations that trigger your partner's anxiety. It will help your partner learn how he or she can tolerate certain levels of anxiety. Your partner will learn how to reduce anxiety and how to manage it in given situations. Over time, you might get surprised how your partner knew to enjoy situations that previously made them anxious.

You have to start with the least challenging situation and progress slowly and steadily towards more challenging ones. Don't push your partner to the next level until they are ready. If anxiety isn't decreasing in the first challenge, it's not time to go to the second. If a situation is causing too much anxiety, and your partner feels they are not ready to deal with it, go back to the previous challenge, and work on it again.

For example, let's say your partner has a fear of heights. They want to overcome this fear and be able to climb the building's last floor. How will exposure therapy look in this case? Tell your partner to look out the window from the ground floor for precisely one minute.

Climb to the second floor together with your partner. Remember that you are not just an exposure therapy guide; you also need to support it. Make them look out the window from the second floor for one minute. If anxiety shows up in its first symptoms, remind your partner to do breathing exercises to lower its impact.

Once your partner feels better, they should try looking out the window again. If no anxiety presents itself, you should leave your partner's side. They need to be able to look through the same window, but this time without you.

Climb to the third floor and repeat steps three and four. When your partner feels ready, continue to the fourth floor, sixth, and so on. If your partner's anxiety is too high, don't hesitate to stop. The first session doesn't need to take longer than 30 minutes.

Each new session needs to begin with the last comfortable floor your partner experienced. You don't need to always start from the ground floor as your partner progresses, feeling no anxiety when looking through the window of the second, third, even fourth floor.

Take time. Your partner will not be free of fear in just a few days. Be patient and continue practicing exposure therapy in this way until your partner can achieve the goal and climb the last floor.

The goal of exposure therapy is not just to get rid of fear and anxiety. It should also teach your partner that they can control and tolerate discomfort. Your partner will have an opportunity to practice anxiety-reduction techniques in a safe and controlled environment with you in the support role.

Plan for relieving your partner's anxiety

Now you know potential techniques you can use to reduce your partner's anxiety. Use this knowledge to create a plan and list practical and ineffective actions when your partner experiences an anxiety attack. It is important to remember what to do in situations that trigger anxiety, but it is also essential to know what not to do.

You and your partner might disagree with what is helpful on the list you are making. It is because your partner craves accommodative behaviors you express when they are under an anxiety attack. Remember that these behaviors relieve anxiety, but in the long run, they do more damage. Try to explain this to your partner. You need to make them understand why such behavior is not suitable for anyone.

Teamwork is beneficial when it comes to fighting a partner's anxiety. But your partner might not want your help due to feelings of shame or think they don't need help. Try making a list on your own. It's worthwhile to do what you can to elevate your partner's anxiety.

The what works list

When making a list of things you can do to help your partner with anxiety, communication is essential. Be specific; question your partner how does it make him feel when you perform particular tasks. How does it feel when you join in breathing exercises? Depending on the personality and level of anxiety, they might even want to be left alone. Maybe they need to be reminded during the panic attack to take short breaths and then perform this task alone.

Choose the right intervention for particular symptoms. Learn to recognize your partner's needs in time and offer help.

Here is an example of an anxiety relief list:

• If I am nervously pacing the room and unable to relax, offer to go outside for a walk with me, or suggest taking a walkout alone.

• If I complain about work without pauses, distract me by choosing a movie we can watch together or suggesting a book I can read alone.

- If I'm obsessing over whether I turned off the iron, reassure me I did and remind me that not repeatedly checking is one step closer to recovering from my OCD.

During a panic attack, fast and shallow breathing is helping me. Remind me how to perform it and join me in this task.

The what doesn't work list

When we love our partner, we feel we will do anything to help them. In our efforts to help, we might not realize that what we are doing is more hurtful. We do mean well, but we don't have experience, patience, or knowledge of what is happening with our partner during an anxiety attack. Sometimes even our partner reinforces us to perform bad tasks for his anxiety in the long run.

It may look complicated, but both you and your partner need to be honest about behaviors that help alleviate anxiety. It will take time and patience to practice to avoid specific actions that bring relief. Here is an example of a "what doesn't work" list:

- I will never again tell my loved one, "just get over it."

- I won't manipulate my partner's feelings to make them stop this behavior.

- I won't use drugs or alcohol to get over my partner's behaviors.

- I won't disrespect my partner's phobias and mock them.

- I won't reinforce my partner's anxiety by accommodating the behavior.

Having a list of what to do and what not to do when anxiety gets triggered will help you and your partner be more in command of your lives. It will stop you from making your partner's anxiety even worse, and it will put both of you on the right track to overcoming the anxiety.

Your relationship will become vibrant, more satisfying, and fulfilling. Anxiety cannot be defeated just by taking the steps on the list. They are just things to do to help your partner overcome fear at that point. You will need to take more severe measures to overcome anxiety fully.

A professional therapist will be of great help. It may take some time to find the right therapist for your partner, and it will take some persistence. Therapists may fit one type of personality but not the other. Be sure your partner is paired with the right therapist, and that will help. Encourage and support your partner, and in time you will learn how to manage their anxiety and possibly even watch them completely overcome it.

Chapter Six

SELF-EVALUATION OF ANXIETY IN A RELATIONSHIP

H ow do you know you are anxious in a relationship? What are the signs that show that you are having a negative emotion concerning your relationship? What are the effects of anxiety on your relationship? All of these questions will be answered when you carry out what is called a self-evaluation of relationship anxiety. This chapter focuses on the self-evaluation of tension in a relationship. The essence of this is to evaluate the issue to put an end to it.

Anxiety can spring out at any time in a relationship. The fact is that everyone is vulnerable to this problem; the tendency to become anxious in a relationship increases as the bond becomes stronger. So, there is a need for everyone to carry out a self-evaluation.

Do you spend most of your time worrying about things that could go wrong in your relationship? Do you doubt if your partner really loves you? A sure sign of relationship anxiety is when you become worried all the time as a result of those questions running through your mind.

For proper self-evaluation of this problem, you need to know the signs that show that you are already becoming anxious. Also, you need to weigh the causes and effects of this problem on your relationship. As I have said earlier, the purpose of evaluating is to address the problem before it develops. This chapter is structured to give you maximum benefit, and I will try to be as explicit as possible.

Signs of anxiety in a relationship

You might be neck-deep in relationship anxiety without really knowing, so this section will point out the symptoms of this problem to you. If you notice any of the signs that will be mentioned below, you will benefit greatly from the self-evaluation process.

1. <u>When you feel jealous of your partner</u>

Take a cursory look at your behavior. Do you feel like breaking somebody's head when your partner is close to the opposite sex? Are you threatened by any friends of theirs who you fear may "steal" your partner away from you? This is jealousy, and it is one of the signs that you are feeling anxious in your relationship. Sometimes, you might even have the urge to test your spouse's commitment and love; this is an indication of anxiety triggered by jealousy.

1. <u>When your self-esteem is low</u>

When you are always cautious of how you behave because you don't know what your partner's reaction will be, or you can't express yourself freely in front of your partner due to fear of rejection, this is an indication of low self-esteem - a sign that you are anxious in your relationship.

1. Lack of trust

Your partner is one of the people you should trust the most. If you always have to confirm whatever your wife, husband, boyfriend, or girlfriend says before you believe them, it shows that there's a lack of trust in the relationship. Many times, the lack of trust is caused by past betrayal. However, you should not allow past betrayals to negatively impact your relationship, provided they were one-time occurrences. Realize that your partner is not perfect, and once they have assured you that such incidences will never happen again, believe them.

1. Emotional imbalance

Today you are frustrated; tomorrow, you are angry; the next day, you are happy – this is emotional instability. You might not be aware of this, but constant mood swings are also a sign of emotional imbalance, and they do not help the matter. They only worsen it. Whatever problems or issues you are facing, discuss them with your partner. When the two of you deliberate on a problem, you will get it solved quickly. When you discover that your mood is not stable, it is a symptom of anxiety in a relationship.

1. Lack of sleep and reduced sex drive

The aftermath of constant worry is insomnia, which is the inability to sleep, and when you are unable to sleep, your body is stressed, leading to decreased libido.

If you are experiencing one or more of these symptoms, you need to figure out the possible causes and deal with them. I am going to give you examples of likely causes of these problems.

Possible causes of a relationship anxiety

Most times, relationship anxiety could be a manifestation of a deep-rooted problem.   Here are the common causes of relationship anxiety:

Complicated Relationship

When you are uncertain about your relationship or not clearly defined, it can be classified as complicated. This applies to those that are dating. For instance, a woman may not know the man's intentions - whether he wants to marry her or is just in it for fun. Also, a long-distance relationship could result in anxiety. In such cases, partners must learn to trust each other.

Comparison

Comparing your current relationship with past ones should be avoided as much as possible. You might begin to entertain feelings of regret if you discover that your previous relationship was better in the areas of finance, communication, sex, and other aspects. To avoid this feeling, you should never compare your marriage or relationship to that of others or the ones you have had in the past.

Constant fighting

When you are always quarreling with your partner, you might never stop worrying because you don't know when the next altercation will crop up. This is one of the causes of severe anxiety in a relationship because your bid to avoid quarreling will not allow you to have a pleasant time with your partner.

Lack of understanding

Partners that do not take the time to understand each other will always face difficulties. As mentioned earlier, the constant quarreling will result in a tense relationship. Are you noticing the symptoms of anxiety coupled with miscommunications? Lack of understanding might be the reason for your relationship anxiety. Get to know your partner better, and encourage them to know you.

Other issues

Difficult experiences in past unhealthy relationships might result in many other issues. Not only that, neglect during childhood, abuse in the past, and lack of affection are some of the reasons why someone can feel anxious in a relationship.

Once you have identified the root cause of your relationship issue, getting rid of it will be the next step. Do not forget, the primary reason for self-evaluating any problem is to get rid of it.

Effects of anxiety

and workarounds

This is a relevant section that you need to read carefully. It opens your eyes to how anxiety manifests in a relationship and the effective ways to stop it no matter how it appears.

Anxiety makes you continuously worry about your relationship

Persistent worry is one of the manifestations of relationship anxiety. If you are continually having thoughts such as, "Is my partner mad at me or are they pretending to be happy with me? Will this relationship last?" These kinds of views indicate one thing – WORRY. If you discover that you regularly entertain these kinds of thought, do the following:

· Clear your mind and live in the moment

· If negative thoughts are continually running through your mind, then stop, clear your mind, and think about the beautiful moments you have shared with your partner. Think about the promises your partner has made, and reassure yourself that your relationship is going to stand the test of time.

· Do not react impulsively - think before you take any step. Share your feelings with your partner rather than withdrawing from them - make an effort to connect.

Anxiety breeds mistrust

Anxiety makes you think negatively about your partner. You will find it difficult to believe anything they say. In some cases, you may suspect that your partner is going out with another person. These kinds of feelings inevitably come between you and your partner, and it makes it hard for you to relate to them well. To put an end to this, follow these practical steps:

· Ask yourself, "Do I have any proof of my suspicion?"

· Go to your partner and talk things over with them

· Start again if you notice that your relationship is suffering from a lack of trust

· Reestablish the trust, date each other as if it is your first time, and gradually build the trust

· Do the things you did when you first met each other

Anxiety leads to self-centeredness

What anxiety does is take all your attention, making you focus solely on the problem while every other thing suffers. You don't have time for your partner; you are withdrawn to yourself. You focus mainly on yourself and neglect the physical and emotional needs of your partner. Here are the things to do to get rid of this attitude:

· Rather than magnifying and focusing on your fear, pay attention to your needs

· You can seek the support of your partner when you discover that you cannot handle the fear alone

Anxiety inhibits expression with your partner

Anything that stops you from expressing your sincere feeling to your partner is an enemy of your relationship. Anxiety is the culprit here; it hinders you from opening your mind to your partner. You think that they might rebuff you or that telling them how you feel may cause an adverse reaction from them. This makes you keep procrastinating instead of discussing the critical issues right away with them. How do you overcome the fear of rejection? Consider the following quick steps:

· Focus on the love your partner has for you

· Voice out what you feel to get rid of anxiety

· Approach your partner cheerfully

· Discuss heartily with them

Anxiety makes you sad

Anxiety breeds these two problems – limitation and fear. A soul battling with these two evils cannot be happy. Anxiety is that culprit that steals your joy by preoccupying you with unnecessary agitation and worry. Happiness is the bedrock of any relationship, so stop being sad and start enjoying happy moments with your partner by taking the following steps:

· Dismiss any thoughts that make you sad

· Play your favorite music to occupy your mind

· Become playful with your partner

· Relive the sweet moments you have had with your partner

· Be humorous, laugh with your partner

Anxiety can either makes you distant or clingy

One way by which you can recognize anxious people is that they tend to be extreme in their actions. If they are not aloof, they will become too attached. Both of these behaviors are extreme and unhealthy. Have you evaluated yourself and discovered that you are guilty of these extremities? Take the action steps below to restore your healthy relationship with your partner:

· Figure out your feelings

· Work on yourself

· Get yourself engaged with things you enjoy doing

Anxiety makes you reject things that will benefit you.

It makes you see everything from one point of view - fear. Anxiety results in indecision in a relationship because you won't know which way is right. Here is how you can stop this problem:

·   Acknowledge your confusing thoughts and deal with them

·   Weigh your decisions carefully without being biased

·   Seek your partner's help if you discover you need support

Strategies to

overcome anxiety

Partners/couples generally face challenges that need to be addressed as the partnership progresses. Your ability to manage issues as they come up in your relationship will ultimately determine its growth. If a challenge is not well managed, you may find your relationship in a crisis and may need to take concrete steps towards charting a way out.

Some of the challenges that most people face in their relationships include:

- communication,
- joint development as a couple,
- relationship needs,
- contentedness and autonomy of the partners,
- equal rights,
- routine,
- habit,
- sexuality,

- loyalty,

- stress,

- quarrels and conflicts,

- the difference in value systems,

- distance, illness,

and the list goes on.

How careful are you in your relationship? Being careful and considerate of each other saves a lot of frustration in the relationship. Do you live in the here and now? Can you enjoy the moment? Living in the here and now sounds easier than it is. More often than not, our thoughts slide into the past or the future.

Other questions to ask yourself about your relationship:

- How intensely are you enjoying the moment?

- Does your partner always understand what you mean?

- Do you do a lot in common together?

- Are both of you a well-rehearsed team in all walks of life?

- Do you find security, tenderness, and sexual satisfaction with your partner?

- How about the division of labor - does it work well between the both of you?

- Do you find peace, support, and security in your relationship?

- Can you talk about everything very openly?

- Does your partner make you strong and happy?

The answers to these questions will guide you into a proper self-evaluation of the challenges you might be facing in your relationship.

In most cases, men do not like relationship talks. Nevertheless, it is necessary to exchange regularly about needs and wishes in a partnership. Especially for conflict resolution, communication strategies are needed. Firstly, you must distinguish between generally communicating as partners and communication as a result of conflict resolution. Communication about each partner's wishes, ideas, plans, and hopes is an important foundation for a relationship. Couples who are happy in long-term relationships are usually able to communicate their feelings to each other, and they do not see themselves or their relationship threatened by these expressions, even if they are negative without being aware of it. They can develop their own very subtle language, gestures, and facial expressions throughout their relationship.

Quarrels are normal in a relationship - it is the "how" that matters. Clashes arise when you or your partner are strained by external stress. For example, a job, problems in raising children, conflicts in the family, etc. The stressed partner often communicates in a more irritated and violent tone.

It is in our greatest interest to be proactive and inventive regarding communicating with those closest to us.

Creating, maintaining, and nurturing relationships with friends, co-workers, and family, not just partners, is critical for our well-being.

The simplest place to start out is with yourself rather than looking to others to create relationship changes.

A relationship self-assessment

Below is a list of some relationship statements. Go through the statements and make notes of any that don't seem to be very true for you. Write these down on a separate sheet of paper.

1. I have told my spouse/partner/children that I really like them within the previous few days or weeks.

2. I get on well with my siblings.

3. I get on well with my coworkers and/or clients.

4. I get on well with my manager and/or employees.

5. There is nobody I might dread or feel uncomfortable running across.

6. I place relationships first and results in second.

7. I have forsaken all of the relationships that drag me down or injury me

8. I have communicated or tried to speak with everybody I may have hurt, injured, or seriously disturbed, though it may not have been 100% my fault.

9. I don't gossip to or about others.

10. I have a circle of friends and/or family who I love and appreciate.

11. I tell people close to me that I appreciate them.

12. I am completely wrapped up in letters, emails, and calls relating to work.

13. I always tell the truth, even if it may hurt.

14. I receive enough love from people around me to feel appreciated.

15. I have forgiven those people that have hurt or broken me, whether or not it was deliberate.

16. I keep my word; people can rely on me.

17. I quickly clear up miscommunications and misunderstandings after they occur.

18. I live life on my terms, not by the principles or preferences of others.

19. There is nothing unresolved with my past loves or spouses.

20. I am in tune with my needs and desires and ensure they are taken care of.

21. I don't judge or criticize others.

22. I have a supporter or lover.

23. I talk openly about issues instead of grumbling.

Problem: money

Many relationship problems start with money. Whether one person manages it differently than the other, or there has been mistrust due to mismanagement of finances in the past, money can strain even the strongest relationship.

Problem-solving strategies:

1. Be honest concerning your current monetary scenario. Don't approach the topic when the situation is tense. Rather, set aside a suitable and convenient time for both of you.

2. Acknowledge the fact that one of you will always be a spender while the other person is a saver, talk about the advantages of each, and try to learn from each other.

3. Do not keep your financial gain or debt away from your partner. If at some point you want to join finances, layout all monetary documents, including recent credit reports, pay stubs, bank statements, insurance policies, debts, and investments.

4. When things go wrong with finances, never apportion blame. Pieces of paper and ones and zeros on a computer are insignificant compared to your human connection.

5. When it comes to shared money, incorporate savings into a joint budget and decide that your monthly bills are a joint responsibility. Still, allow the both of you to be independent by putting aside some money to be spent when the need arises.

6. Make decisions concerning your long-term as well as short-term goals. It's normal to have personal goals, but you must not underestimate the importance of family goals.

Problem: Struggles over home chores

A majority of partners work outside the house and sometimes at more than one job. Therefore, it is vital to fairly divide the household responsibilities.

Problem-solving strategies:

1. Be organized and clear regarding your jobs within the home. Write all the roles down and agree on who will do what or what schedule to work off of. Be honest about what you do or do not want to do and what you have time for.

2. Be open to alternative solutions: If you each hate housework, perhaps you'll be able to spring for a cleaning service. Or maybe you can be a bit laxer about the level of cleanliness around the house. If you're a neat freak, but your partner isn't, is there a compromise to be found? Always make an effort to meet in the middle.

Problem: Not prioritizing your relationship

If you wish to keep your relationship going, prioritizing your relationship is a must. Make it meaningful and worth your while. Recognize its importance, cherish it, and nourish it so that it will stand the test of time.

Problem-solving strategies:

1. Go back to those things you did when you started dating. Appreciate one another, give compliments, contact one another through the day, and show genuine interest in each other.

2. Schedule a time to go on a date and plan it with as much consideration as to when you were trying to win each other over.

3. Respect is fundamental. Learn to be appreciative. If your partner does something that makes you happy, never

hesitate to show your gratitude by saying thank you. Let your partner know what matters most to you - them.

Problem: Conflict

Occasional conflict is a part of life. However, if you and your partner are constantly arguing, it is time to break the cycle and be freed from this poisonous routine. Instead of getting angry, look carefully into underlying problems and find ways to solve the issue without hostility.

Problem-solving strategies:

1. You and your partner will learn to argue in an exceedingly civil, useful manner.

2. Realize you're not a victim - it's your choice if you react the way you do. Be honest with yourself and with your partner about how you feel.

3. Once you are in the middle of an argument, pay attention to how you phrase things and the tone of your voice. Would you be okay with your partner speaking to you the way you're speaking to them? Put love and kindness first, and never forget that the person you're arguing with is also the person you've chosen to spend your life with. Is the conflict worth more than the relationship?

4. If you still respond with the kind of approach that has brought you pain and unhappiness within the past, you cannot expect a different result at this point. For example, if you were in the habit of interrupting your partner before they are done talking because you want to defend yourself, hold off for some moments. You will be shocked at how such

a change in tempo will have a remarkable effect on the tone of an argument.

5. Give a little, get heaps. Apologize when you are wrong. It's a powerful way to show your partner that you value them above being right. Try it and see the amazing result.

6. You cannot manage another person's behavior; you must not fail to acknowledge the fact that you are only in charge of yourself.

Problem: Trust

Trust is vital as far as relationship is concerned. Are you always seeing things that make your trust for your partner dwindle? Or do you have issues that are not yet resolved, making you not trust other people?

Problem-solving strategies:

You and your partner will develop trust in one another by considering the following pointers.

- Always be consistent.
- Be on time.
- Never fail to do what you have promised to do.
- Don't tell a lie -- not even a white lie to your lover or any other person.
- Be fair, even in an argument.
- Be sensitive to the other's feelings. You'll still disagree, however, do not discount how your partner is feeling.
- Call when you say you'll.

- Call to mention you will be home late.

- Carry your weight and fulfill promises and responsibilities.

- Never say things you cannot take back.

- Don't reopen old wounds.

- Have regard for your partner's boundaries.

- Avoid being needlessly jealous.

- Always be realistic.

Thinking your partner can meet all of your wants -- and will be able to figure them out without your saying anything -- might be closer to a Hollywood fantasy. Ask for what you would like directly.

You should be ever ready to make your relationship work and to really look into what must be done. Do not conclude that you can't enjoy a peaceful and loving relationship with another person until you have looked over all the conflicts and attempted to address them. Unless you attend to the issues in your current relationship, any future relationships will be marred by the same problems.

Chapter Seven

INSECURITY AND SELF ESTEEM

I nsecurities about relationships are highly frequent, and most people have felt insecure at some point in their lives. When these insecurities become chronic, they can negatively affect your most intimate relationships and daily life.

Having significant relationship insecurities robs you of your capacity for peace. It will make you feel uneasy or inauthentic in the presence of your significant other. Interestingly, most relationship insecurities stem from within rather than from how or what your partner does.

These emotions are frequently instilled early, possibly due to attachment issues with one's parents or family members. They may also appear to be hurt by a prior lover or rejected by someone you loved intensely. Most relationship anxieties are the result of erroneous thoughts. Perhaps you believe that you are unworthy, that you will be nothing without your spouse, that no one will truly love you, or that you will never find another.

If any of this rings true for you, have no fear—we've compiled some simple ideas and tactics to assist you in managing these concerns.

A trust-based relationship

Simply put, healthy relationships cannot exist without a high level of trust. However, almost all of us have encountered instances in our lives when trust has been violated in a relationship, whether through something as innocuous as a white lie or as serious as adultery.

It is critical to avoid bringing these feelings of distrust from former partners into a new relationship with a partner who has never given you a reason to be suspicious of them.

Trust is difficult to earn but extremely quick to lose, so it is critical to work consistently and again. You must be willing to believe your partner unless they demonstrate otherwise.

Several key methods for increasing trust include the following:

- Exchange of information
- Consulting with others before making any decisions
- Being congruent with one another
- Respect for your commitments
- Active listening
- Being truthful
- Acknowledging errors

- Being candid about your emotions

All these strategies can be used to build trust in a relationship, but they only work when both parties are prepared to commit. It is critical to recognize when a partner makes these attempts and to make an effort to meet them halfway.

Troubling signs and solutions

With our increased access to social media, insecurity is rampant in relationships. This is not to say, however, that relationship insecurity should take over your life. There are several things you can do to assist in resolving the situation. But first, here are some symptoms that your relationship is insecure.

1. You desire to examine your partner's phone. Your partner leaves the sofa to take a shower and forgets to take their phone with them. What are your responsibilities? If your initial instinct was to check it and see who they were speaking with, you might be experiencing relationship insecurity. While it may appear to be harmless, it is a clear violation of their privacy.

2. You disapprove of their social life. If you're concerned about your partner seeing their pals at the park, this is a significant indicator of distrust and insecurity. If you can't accept your partner seeing friends without fear of them cheating on you, it's time to confront your insecurities.

3. You steer clear of conflict. We are not proposing that constant argument is beneficial, but if you keep things within and avoid discussing them, there will eventually be a blow-up. One key indicator of insecurity is avoiding complex topics when they are required for an excellent intimate connection.

Effects on insecurity on the couple

While you may believe that you will be OK if you keep your insecurities to yourself and away from your partner, this is unfortunately not the case. Eventually, these feelings will seep through, whether via words or deeds, wreaking havoc on your relationship.

1. Have faith in your significant other. Trust is the cornerstone of any successful relationship. Any love connection is built on the foundation of trust. Without complete confidence in your spouse, you may wind up pushing them away or struggling to open up emotionally, impeding the relationship's development over time.

2. You act on bad thoughts. Everyone has negative thoughts; it is an unavoidable aspect of life. However, if you constantly bombard yourself with negative thoughts, they will eventually get internalized, affecting your behavior. These activities will also have a detrimental influence on your relationship as a whole.

3. You are constantly in need of reassurance. Again, everyone occasionally needs some reassurance. If, on the other hand, you require constant confirmation, something is badly wrong.

Apart from that, as your partner grows bored of your constant need for reassurance, you will become even more insecure. This type of behavior must be corrected immediately.

Practical tips to overcome insecurity

Therefore, how can you overcome some of these insecurities and allow your relationship to flourish? Here are some straightforward life principles that will help you overcome some of your insecurities.

1. Keep in mind that not everything revolves around you. Primarily, it's critical to take a step back and recognize that not everything is about you. If your partner declines to join you on a night out, this does not necessarily mean they do not wish to be seen with you. It's more than likely that they're exhausted and don't feel like going out.

2. Avoid becoming paranoid for no reason. Girls have male pals, while males have female friends. After all, the year is 2020. Simply because your partner has friends of the opposing sex does not suggest they are cheating on you or are anything other than the friends your partner claims to have.

3. Do not shy away from confrontation. By confronting issues head-on and discussing them until they are resolved, you will create a level of trust with your partner that is so strong that you will feel comfortable discussing anything and everything with them. This is ultimately worth the difficult initial chats.

4. Eliminate your reliance on others. Self-love is the most critical kind of love. Having this in place before venturing into the realm of dating is critical if you desire long and lasting partnerships. While Hugs and kisses are wonderful, it's critical to first love yourself and trust that you'll be fine if these things ever go away.

Can I overcome my fear?

Now that we've established some of the critical characteristics of insecurity let's look at some simple suggestions and tactics for overcoming those negative thoughts and behaviors.

1. Increase your sense of self-worth. Self-esteem enhancement will go a long way toward eliminating insecurities in your relationship. By investing the time to do so, you will increase your confidence and trustworthiness. Taking a personal day, visiting a spa, or exercising more frequently are all fantastic ways to boost self-esteem.

2. Have confidence in your relationship and yourself. Simply put, trust equals happiness. Trust is the foundation of healthy relationships because it enables your partner to live their life and blossom. Additionally, it is critical to trust your instincts. If your partner has never cheated on you or given you cause to believe they would, why would you be suspicious of them?

3. Develop the ability to stop overthinking. Finally, it is critical to avoid overthinking. Take it in stride if your partner decides to see some friends without you. Overthinking these seemingly innocuous human behaviors can result in additional doubt and

suspicion for no cause. It is critical to recognize when you are doing this and to instantly block this sensation.

Attempt to avoid allowing fear to destroy your relationship

A little fear in a relationship is beneficial! Fear of losing your significant other reaffirms how strongly you care about your mate. Additionally, it demonstrates your level of concern. However, having too much dread in a relationship might eventually destroy it—but it does not have to.

Communicating with your partner is one method to address your worries in a relationship. By sharing your concerns with your partner, you enable them access to your thinking and provide them with a greater knowledge of how you think. Additionally, you should be present to listen to your partner's anxieties. You may even be shocked to discover that they share many of your issues!

There are also several sorts of fear, like fear of loneliness, boredom, and change, to name a few. It is critical to recognize which concerns are significant to you because this will enable you to confront them more effectively in the future.

By addressing your relationship fears collaboratively, you're taking the initial steps toward developing trust and elevating your partnership.

Adapting your relationship to fear

After effectively identifying the anxieties that exist in your relationship, the effort does not end there. It is critical to keep these fears in check. Ensure that you discuss them as necessary. Keep a lid on them to avoid them having a bad impact on your relationship in the future.

By establishing a solid and trustworthy relationship foundation, you will feel at ease calling each other out on fear-based acts or feelings. This will enable both of you to manage your worries while still progressing in your relationship. Over time, these relationship worries will be eased by the two of you taking continuous good action. Fear will diminish as the relationship progresses—but only if these firm foundations are established initially.

As an analogy, consider the construction of a house. When constructing a house, one does not begin with the roof. You begin by constructing the foundations, followed by the walls and structural supports, and finally, the roof. Only when the initial foundation work is completed will you know whether you have a robust and durable house.

Chapter Eight

COUPLE CONFLICT

Unsurprisingly, many married couples suffer quite similar challenges, most of which are resolvable, avoidable, or repairable.

1. Sexual differences: While some may find it awkward to admit it, the physical connection is necessary for long-lasting partnerships. As a result, sexual incompatibility and libido loss are common problems for married couples.

2. Beliefs and values: There will always be disagreements in a marriage, which is perfectly normal. It is beneficial to engage in debates and conversations about a variety of subjects. Unfortunately, some distinctions are simply too great to ignore. These are frequently referred to as an individual's beliefs or values. These are frequently neglected or neglected during the early stages of a relationship, but they can develop into severe marital problems over time.

3. Life stages: While this subject is frequently disregarded in discussions about relationships, the issue of life stages is

pervasive, particularly in our modern, fast-paced culture. Occasionally, the basis of marital conflict is a partner's desire for something else in life. These difficulties are especially prevalent in partnerships between couples with a substantial age difference.

4. Stress: This one occurs at least once in almost every marriage. Stress can be triggered by various factors, including familial, mental health, or financial concerns. How this stress is managed can greatly impact the importance of this issue in a marriage.

Issues that put even happy marriages at risk

Issues are not exclusive to people in bad marriages; they can also bother even the healthiest of couples. However, the distinction between successful and terrible marriages is in how these issues are addressed and how much each partner permits the issue to escalate before resolving it. Even in a good marriage, one issue that frequently rears its ugly head is overstepping boundaries.

According to studies, once a couple marries, it is not rare for one of the spouses to switch partners. This could be anything from their values to their appearance—the spouse tries to modify their spouse.

These attempts can create friction between the relationship, which can become destructive if left unresolved. Infidelity can also manifest itself emotionally in a loving marriage. Thus, even if there is no physical adultery, emotional adultery can occur when two people drift apart and develop relationships with persons outside the marriage.

It's sometimes comforting to know that even individuals in successful marriages can encounter difficulties. This can help put your relationship concerns into context and allow you to be a bit kinder to yourself.

Relationship mistakes

Everybody makes mistakes in relationships, even those that last a long time. Expecting that neither you nor your partner will ever make a relationship error is unreasonable. Maintaining an unreasonable standard can result in undue pressure on a relationship, resulting in totally different challenges.

The severity of errors varies. Some can be fixed with time and dialogue, while others are difficult to recover from. Taking your mate for granted is a typical relationship error. As a relationship matures and deepens, it's natural to fall into a new life routine.

That is all well and good. However, partners can get overly comfortable, to the point that they begin to take their significant other for granted. Another error that some people make as relationships progress is to remove their privacy boundaries.

At first, a deep relationship is built through protecting each other's best-kept secrets and developing a reputation as a trustworthy source of information for your spouse. However, if these secrets are gradually revealed to close friends and family, they might introduce additional concerns of trust and anxiety into the relationship.

Money conflicts

As a relationship develops, your lives become increasingly entwined. This is a wonderful thing since it connects each spouse into the lives of the other, allowing for the sharing of additional memories. These memories include vacations, pets, automobile purchases, and even homeownership. All these milestones are critical and vital for a relationship, but they also bring financial concerns.

Occasionally, conflicts can occur as a result of a partner's excessive spending habits. You may get uncomfortable with their expenditures on stuff such as clothing, shoes, and other non-essential stuff.

Another difficulty that can arise in a money-related relationship is the question of saving money. You may have divergent views on how much money you should save each week, which might result in arguments on how to save money. Again, it is critical to discuss these problems to better understand how your partner thinks and why they feel differently about saving than you do. You will then be able to establish mutually beneficial savings goals that will hopefully suit the objectives of both parties.

Defending one's point of view determinately

In any relationship, it is critical to stand up for what you believe in. If you abandon your principles and convictions to keep your partner happy and avoid conflict, you will eventually find yourself unhappy and apprehensive about the relationship.

Someone's perspective and opinions are a significant element of what makes each of us unique. It's also quite possible that this is one of the primary reasons your spouse fell for you in the first place. As a result, it's critical to understand how to defend oneself without coming across as defensive to maintain your points of view intact.

When expressing your viewpoint on a subject, ensure that you have conducted sufficient study. When you offer an idea, some will always concur, but there will also always be those who disagree.

Additionally, ensure that you are open to constructive criticism. It is one thing to express verbal gratitude. However, by demonstrating that you are absorbing information, you demonstrate to your partner that you are willing to listen and learn and that they should be as well. Possessing a strong point of view also necessitates a great deal of patience. It's possible that your partner initially does not understand, and that's fine. Be prepared to stick to your guns, and they will eventually understand how critical that specific subject is to you.

Crisis, the road to divorce

"Crisis" is a large term that should only be used when absolutely essential! As a result, it is critical to address these possible concerns before they escalate into a crisis resulting in divorce.

1. Libido loss: It's pointless to pretend that sex isn't a significant element of any relationship. If you allow it, your sex life in marriage can deteriorate with time. As a result, it is critical to have a good sexual relationship with your spouse. Communicate your preferences and dissatisfactions. Continue to instill the desire in your partner through your acts and words.

2. Emotional or physical infidelity: Both emotional and physical infidelity are difficult to overcome if left unresolved. Physically cheating on someone is a difficult step to overcome in some situations, resulting in divorce in others. Additionally, knowing that your partner has cheated on you emotionally or physically might result in increased levels of tension and worry.

3. Financial disagreements: Another difficulty that can emerge throughout the marriage is financial disagreements. These might stem from a variety of factors, including how money is spent or saved. These conflicts may begin modest at first, but they can escalate into additional anger if not addressed thoroughly.

Two couples' secret sexual issues

Finally, disagreements between spouses over sexual concerns boil down to two major concerns. These two issues are more prevalent than you might believe, and how you resolve them as a couple is critical to the relationship's continued growth and prosperity.

Firstly, there is frequently one partner who is dissatisfied with the amount of sex in the relationship. This could be a partner who wishes they had more sex together or a spouse who wishes they made love less frequently. Without being addressed, this irritation may breed additional hatred over time.

This can become a problem that spreads to other areas of the relationship, so it's critical to halt the spread of these difficulties by early communication. It will enable partners to understand one another before moving forward with the relationship. This leads us to our second point, communication. Couples frequently struggle to communicate what they appreciate and dislike in the bedroom.

This can occasionally result in a less pleasurable and intimate bedroom experience, impeding the entire relationship's advancement.

Couples' common concerns

1. How do I know they're the ones?

It can be tough to determine whether someone is "the one" for you at times. Regrettably, some friends make it appear so clear with their relationship that it causes you to doubt your own sentiments. Remember that everyone's emotions are unique, and your relationship cannot be compared to another. As a result, determining whether someone is the one is difficult. However, if you like spending time with your partner and envision a future together, this is typically a positive indicator.

2. I am not yet prepared to marry, but my partner is.

This is pretty frequent and makes a lot of sense when you think about it. How likely are you and your partner to be in the same emotional place at the same time? If your spouse is a good match for you, they will respect your viewpoint and wait patiently for you to mature in your own time.

3. I have the impression that my partner does not trust me.

This can be a challenging situation and must be handled cautiously. To begin, it's worthwhile to discuss this emotion with your partner, explaining why you're feeling this way. This enables your spouse to address why they may lack faith in you or why they are unwilling to alter their conduct. It will serve as a beginning point for adjusting your relationship as necessary.

Solving conflicts tips

Conflict is an unavoidable component of nearly all relationships. Additionally, it can be a significant source of stress. As a result, it is critical to resolve most confrontations. This may seem self-evident, but many people hide their anger or simply 'go along to get along.' Some believe that they are actually creating one by resolving a disagreement and hence prefer to remain silent while angered. Regrettably, this is not a sustainable long-term plan. Unresolved disagreement in a relationship can breed resentment and further unresolved conflict. Even more concerning, the persistent dispute can have a detrimental effect on one's health and longevity.

Regrettably, overcoming disagreements can also be challenging. When handled correctly, attempts at mediation can actually exacerbate the issue. For instance, John Gottman and his colleagues investigated how couples fight and discovered that they could predict which couples will divorce based on their conflict resolution skills—or lack thereof.

Couples who continuously attack their partner's character or withdraw during disagreements should be on their guard rather than resolving the dispute in a proactive, polite manner.

For individuals who were not born into a home where excellent conflict resolution skills were demonstrated regularly (and, let's face it, how many of us were?), here are some principles for simplifying and de-stressing dispute resolution.

Connect with your emotions

A critical component of conflict resolution includes simply— understanding how and why you feel the way you do. While it may appear that your feelings should be self-evident, this is not always the case. At times, you may feel angry or bitter for no apparent reason. In other instances, you may feel as though the other person is not doing what they 'should,' but you are unsure of what you want from them or whether your request is even realistic.

Journaling can be an excellent approach to connect with your own emotions, thoughts, and expectations to transmit them more effectively to the other person.

Occasionally, this process brings up some quite serious concerns, for which counseling may be beneficial.

<u>Develop your listening ability</u>

When it comes to effective dispute resolution, listening skills are at least as crucial as speaking skills. It is critical to grasp the other person's perspective in addition to our own if we are to reach an agreement. Indeed, simply assisting the other person in feeling heard and understood can frequently go a long way toward resolving a problem. Additionally, effective listening enables you to bridge the divide between the two of you, identify the source of the disconnect, and so forth.

Unfortunately, active listening is a skill that not everyone possesses, and it is common for people to believe they are listening while in fact crafting their next reaction, thinking to themselves how wrong the other person is, or engaging in other activities unrelated to attempting to grasp the other person's perspective. Additionally, it is common to be so defensive and nestled in your own perspective that you cannot hear another person.

Develop assertive communication skills

Communicating your feelings and needs openly is also critical in resolving conflicts. As you are surely aware, saying the incorrect thing can exacerbate a quarrel. What's critical to remember is to express yourself clearly and assertively, without being confrontational or putting the other person on the defensive.

One effective method for resolving conflict is to express yourself in terms of how you feel, rather than what you believe the other person is doing incorrectly, by utilizing 'I feel' phrases.

Look for a resolution

Once you've gained an understanding of the other person's perspective and they've gained an understanding of yours, it's time to resolve the conflict—a solution that both parties can live with. Occasionally, a simple and obvious solution emerges when both parties grasp the other's perspective. When a quarrel results from misunderstanding or a lack of understanding of the other's perspective, a simple apology can work wonders, and an open discussion can bring people together.

In other instances, a bit more effort is required. When two people disagree on a topic, you have a few options: Occasionally, you may agree to disagree, occasionally, you may reach a compromise or a middle ground, and occasionally, the person who feels more strongly about an issue may get their way with the understanding that they will concede the next time. The critical point is to understand and attempt to resolve issues in a respectful manner of all parties concerned.

<u>Recognize when it isn't working</u>

Due to the toll that ongoing disagreement may exact on an individual, it is often prudent to maintain some distance in a relationship or to cut ties completely.

Simple conflict resolution tactics will only go you so far in times of abuse, and personal safety must take precedence.

On the other side, when dealing with challenging family members, putting a few limits and respecting the other person's limits in the relationship can bring about some calm. In unsupportive friendships or those marked by chronic conflict, letting go can be a significant source of stress alleviation. Only you can determine whether a relationship can be improved or if it should be terminated.

Chapter Nine

MANAGE YOUR EXPECTATIONS

I t's not bad to have expectations of your partner. You should have expectations of your partner just as your partner should have expectations of you. Expectations let you both know what you need out of one another to keep the relationship functioning as it should. It's okay to expect your partner to take you out to dinner when they say they will or pick up the kids from school, as you agreed upon.

Often, well-established negotiations of who does what keep the chaos under control and allow households to flow more smoothly; however, couples often have unrealistic and damaging expectations of each other. When you have these crazy expectations of your partner (or of yourself), you're setting your relationship up for failure and hurting yourself in the process.

The truth about expectations

There are some common expectations that couples have going into relationships and because of societal expectations. For example, men are often viewed as providers, while women are expected to manage household tasks and arrange for childcare. Even women who work are expected to, by default, handle childcare.

More than 40% of working women in America, according to a survey by the Center for American Progress, said that childcare problems were detrimental to their careers as opposed to their male counterparts. In families where both partners work, the mother's expectation of making career sacrifices is often still in place, damaging relationships. Likewise, a male who makes less of an income and therefore decides to stay home with the kids may be judged by outsiders for not being the provider he is expected to be. For all genders, these expectations place undue stress on people.

While those gendered expectations are external from the relationship, they often do become internalized by couples. Women may feel lots of pressure from their husbands to take care of the children while balancing careers. In contrast, men may feel lots of pressure to make more money and provide for their families while still being emotionally and physically present during off-hours.

These scenarios can pass gender lines and be important to same-sex couples as well. In any case, expectations from society can then cause fights and dysfunction in your relationship. You may find yourself having expectations simply because they've been passed down to you through the generations, which means there are expectations that you need to evaluate and determine whether they fit your relationship.

Personal dangerous expectations

Beyond societal expectations, you may have damaging expectations that are specific to your relationship. You may expect perfection from your partner, especially in areas you deem their domain. If your partner is good at a particular household task, you may expect them always to complete that task even though you are perfectly capable of achieving that task. When your partner is washing the dishes, you may see an unsightly streak and yell at them for ten minutes about how they washed that dish. You might get angry when your partner is late coming home from work, even if they have a good excuse. These are examples of unrealistic expectations that cause your relationship to deteriorate. Your partner won't always do things the way you want to be done, and they won't still maintain your standard, and that's okay because they aren't meant to be just like you. They are different people, so to expect them to be the ideal version of yourself won't do anything.

When you have such high expectations, your partner will struggle to keep up with your demands. They will feel like they can never please you and think they are failing you. By having high expectations, you will not only fuel your anxiety, but you will also fuel theirs. The anxiety that bubbles up, as a result, will cause passive-aggressive behaviors or fighting.

Finally, when you hold someone else to such high standards, you have to hold yourself to that same standard to avoid being a hypocrite. You have no choice but to put impossible standards on yourself as well. Keeping to those standards is exhausting.

You will be exhausted, your partner will be exhausted, and your relationship will not be the supportive haven that you both need to recharge and feel good about yourselves.

How to maintain reasonable expectations

You have the right to expect certain things from your partners like respect, love, support, and safety, but most else, you can't just expect to have without talking about your expectations. Make it clear the household duties and romantic gestures you expect from your partner. Don't make them guess because if you aren't clear about what you want, you can't expect anyone to meet your standard.

Be clear about the things you need your partner to do. Suppose you need something from your partner, outline why you need it and how you expect it to be accomplished. In this process, try not to be too overbearing and demanding. Remember that your partner is still their person and doesn't need to be micromanaged, but if it's important to you that certain things be done a certain way, you can ask your partner if they would be okay with doing it that way.

For example, suppose you like to keep your favorite pan in one cupboard, and your partner always puts it in another. In that case, that's something you should discuss rather than expecting that your partner is putting the pan in the other location to bother you. Little incidents like that sound silly, but if you've been in a long-term relationship, you know that it's those little things that can set you off and get a long-awaited fight going.

Don't expect your significant other to read your mind. Your partner may know you well, but they can't know everything that you want or need. Don't try to convey your wants in riddles or try to drop cryptic hints. If you expect you and your partner to go out to dinner on your anniversary, tell your partner what you want. Your partner doesn't have to comply. You can't expect always to get your way, but if what you want is reasonable, someone who loves you will probably try to make it work unless it would be harmful to them.

Know your partner's limits. If your partner is afraid of heights, don't expect them to go skydiving just because you asked that of them. Know that just like you have fears, traumas, and limits, your partner does too. They are not superhuman, and you can't expect them to do something out of character or terrifying. You and your significant other need to feel secure in your relationship, and you can't do that if you're making insane demands that make them markedly uncomfortable. It's good for partners to push each other's limits and encourage each other to do new things, but you should do so, keeping your partner's needs and wants in mind.

Be flexible. Life is incredibly dynamic. Situations alter in the blink of an eye, so be prepared that one day your expectations might be reasonable, and the next day, they might be unreasonable. For example, your partner loses their job. Maybe you generally expect a very nice birthday gift, but that expectation has to shift based on new economic circumstances in this situation. In that case, most partners would understand when they received a smaller birthday gift, but if you don't shift your expectations, you're in for a bad surprise when you open that smaller present! Being flexible also means knowing that sometimes unexpected events happen. Your partner won't always be at their best, and sometimes they will make mistakes. They'll forget your anniversary or make the food you hate for dinner. Don't take those mistakes personally.

People have a lot going on at any given time, and the mistake probably has to do more with everything else rather than being a reflection upon their love and devotion to you. Suppose your partner starts repetitively making these mistakes. In that case, it's time to start questioning your relationship. Still, it's normal to make such slip-ups every so often, and you've probably made plenty of similar mistakes in the relationship too.

Don't expect too much of yourself, either. Sometimes your harmful expectations in a relationship can be ones you place on yourself. Just as putting unrealistic expectations on your partner is harmful, holding yourself to such a high standard is also harmful. Don't be hard on yourself if you sometimes mess up. Emotions and a lack of knowledge can make it hard to deal with certain situations, and accordingly, it's easy to mess up and do things that hurt your partner or disappoint them.

Nevertheless, it's not the end of the world or your relationship. You weren't perfect, but that doesn't detract from your worth or make you any less loved by your partner. It's time to move on and accept that, sometimes, the unexpected occurs, and all you can do is your best.

It's okay to ask your partner to make changes but do so with caution. There are some things in a relationship that, for whatever reason, you cannot stand. Perhaps, you hate when your partner pops their gum because it sends a surge of annoyance through you. It's okay to bring the things that bother you up to your partner and even ask your partner to make changes, but you can't expect them to change.

When you have such a talk, be sure to listen to any counterpoints your partner may have. Or, if your partner starts such a discussion with you, try not to jump straight to being angry and remember that they're discussing their feelings, which are not a personal attack on you. When someone is annoyed with you, it isn't necessarily because you're doing something wrong, but it is often because of the other person's insecurities and worries. Thus, think of such discussions as constructive rather than an attack on your character.

Also, remember that it can be harmful to pressure any person to change. Don't give ultimatums, and don't try to manipulate them into changing. In many cases, all you can do is express your feelings and hope to mutually conclude how to handle that situation.

If you can, find people to help you with duties that become too overwhelming. Maybe you're both having trouble balancing your housework. If you can afford one, find a housecleaner. Alternatively, pay a babysitter one night so that you and your partner can go out and spend some quality time with each other or send the kids to spend time with their grandparents. Don't expect the people in your life to help you, but if you're in need and feeling like you can't manage it all, the people in your life can likely provide you some help, even if it's just a shoulder to cry on or an open ear to listen to all your concerns.

When establishing good expectations, the essential thing to remember is that all you both can do is your best. Be aware that you both have flaws, and accordingly, not everything you expect will be possible. Additionally, surprises and normal life issues such as the death of a loved one or struggling finances may require you to reevaluate your expectations and be open to new ones.

Chapter Ten

DEALING WITH JEALOUSY

One of the fundamental reasons for jealousy originates from a period in an individual's life when emotional damage is done, which assaults their reality or, eventually, their feelings of internal security. These instabilities will truly influence a woman's confidence, which will bring about feelings of low self-esteem and doubt, eliminating any sense of pride.

Emotional wounds

These emotional injuries can be brought about by physical and mental abuse and traumas or an over-prohibitive or dominated adolescence. If a child is sexually assaulted, their security is compromised through confiding in the offender. Quite often, the child grows up feeling guilty for what happened to them. This is also validated when she's an adult and still feels responsible.

When a child is mentally abused, they normally carry on long-suffering verbal abuse and degrading. It happens to grown-ups in their relationships as well. The over-prohibitive or dominating childhood starts in early adolescence and follows through into adulthood. These abuses transform into profound emotional wounds.

These wounds will make a person feel like they're in a prison of anxiety and instability. If they don't learn to classify them, execute them, and make them stronger, they'll never be free of them. Women often look for explanations to tackle the issue that they feel within themselves, continually achieving nothing.

They don't look for it in themselves. This is the mistake they make because they have several issues.

The human brain is made of two halves, which permits two different ways of reasoning—positive and negative. Unfortunately, as mentioned before, if an individual is abused or loses trust, it weakens their capacity to keep the balance between them. This is when they'll be the victim of specific causes that will flare up the thing that prompts jealousy. You might be considering what these causes are. They are something like a recollection from the past. It can be a smell, an individual's laughter, an image, another woman, a feeling of dismissing, or a memory of your partner looking at you. There is a wide range of causes that can bring about negative feelings.

Managing negative emotions

Negative relationship factors are distinct causes. It happens when a relationship severs because of trust issues brought about by unfaithfulness or sex addiction by one partner. This will follow them into each subsequent relationship if they can't get in control of their problems.

Jealousy isn't a problem that can be overlooked or pardoned. You should fear jealousy because fear is what makes it a negative inclination. Have you, at any point, seen how quickly jealousy can change your relationship from cheerful to destructive? It's one of the worst feelings, and nobody would ever wish it on anyone, even one they dislike.

The negative emotions hiding behind jealousy will slowly reduce your love and change it to fraud, dishonesty, and hate. It will make you change from a happy person to someone overly suspicious and running away from the truth. Reality is jealousy's enemy. Jealousy always averts reality, even faster than it changes the positive thoughts to negative ones. It controls your mind and makes you think that a person you have a strong feeling for is not who they used to be. It makes you believe that they are a cheater, want someone else, watch adult videos without your knowledge, never tell you the truth, and misunderstand what you say to them, so you make a fool of yourself. They will laugh at you when you're begging for help. It'll make you feel really bad until you feel like vomiting, and it'll make you uncertain. It makes your body feel different. You may break out into a sweat and cause your breathing to become rapid. If you've ever felt this way, I'm pretty sure that you know what I'm talking about.

This negative feeling will make you dread abandonment. This fear is a strong trigger to jealousy. It will capture and force you into suffocating or protecting what belongs to you until that individual can never again be hurt because of your jealousy. It'll make you feel a profound desire to manipulate everything your partner thinks and does.

Enabling jealousy to make your mind want to manipulate it is a sign of addiction. In this connection prison, your fragileness makes your relationship weak. You have to feel appended, and it'll consume the feeling of being secure and affect your self-esteem. A perfect illustration of a connection prison is fear of letting your partner out of your sight, such as not letting him go to work because you're afraid he'll meet someone and leave you for them.

Jealousy is like medication. When you let it get to you, you can't control it anymore. You let it control you. You have now become a dependent thinker, subject to jealousy and power. Having desires like this is like an addict requiring drugs.

Jealousy is your addiction, and the adrenaline of being scared makes you feel like you're high. However, this isn't positive adrenaline; it's an unadulterated negative adrenaline surge. The primary antidote to battle it is with some positive steps to reinforce your capacity to reclaim your control and get free from that jail.

Jealousy won't rest until it makes a disappointing and intolerable condition that makes you the cause of the problems in your relationship. In actuality, you've become the aggressor that you never wanted to be. You're jealous now! You're the reason for the unrest tossed into the world outside you. It's a world that can't, in any way, shape, or form, sympathize with your torment. You have nobody else but you in this jail. You're the only person able to feel the agony, the one in particular whose desires are controlling the situation and avoiding the world. You will wind up being consumed by negative considerations every time you turn around.

The path to overcoming jealousy

Ending jealousy is like altering every mental or behavioral response. It begins with consciousness. Awareness lets you see that the stories are not real in your head. If you are so straightforward, you no longer respond to the possibilities that your imagination might imagine.

Jealousy and anger are emotional reactions that are not true in believing situations in your head. You should change what you think affects your imagination and remove these harmful emotional reactions. Even if the response is warranted, envy and rage are not good ways to cope with the situation to get what we want. Trying to change anxiety or resentment is like controlling a car skidding on ice. Your ability to deal with the situation will significantly improve if you can avoid the risk before you get there. This means addressing the beliefs that cause jealousy rather than trying to control your emotions.

Dissolving relationships permanently means changing the underlying beliefs of fear and unconscious expectations of what your partner is doing.

The steps to end jealous reactions permanently are:

1. Recover personal power so that you can control your emotions and stop reactive behavior.

2. Change your point of view so you can step back from your plot.

3. Be mindful that your convictions are not valid; this is distinct from scientifically "knowing" that the claims are not real.

4. Gain power over your focus so that you can actively select your mind's story and emotions.

Several factors establish the envy dynamic. Practical solutions will tackle multiple elements of values, experiences, feelings, and strength of personal will. You will leave the doors open to those negative emotions and behaviors if you lack one or more of these components.

You can step back from the story by practicing some simple exercises and refrain from being caught up in the emotional reaction. If you want to change your feelings and actions, you can do it. It only takes some willingness to acquire sufficient skills.

Chapter Eleven

NARCISSISTIC ABUSE IN RELATIONSHIPS

As much as you might have heard or read about narcissists, you are not necessarily wrong to build a relationship with one. You also need to know that you are not deliberately setting yourself on the path of self-destruction. Narcissists are quite romantic and can be charming. They are great lovers and can be friends. The truth is that they can be sensitive to how you feel and adjust to your needs.

Narcissism and manipulation

However, narcissists can be very manipulative, and they are complicated people. Therefore, being in any sort of relationship, whether romantic or not, spiritual or professional, you need to know that it can be confusing, and you need to be prepared for the situation. Narcissists are complicated and sometimes hard to understand. You will find them very helpful and dependable to the point they will seem to care about you. The truth is their devotion and kindness are mostly to benefit themselves and further put them in control of things.

Forming a relationship with a narcissist is not uncommon. Many people are in a narcissistic relationship without even realizing it until they are too far into it. The victim often doesn't feel like leaving because his or her life is centered on the narcissist. It is difficult to let go of such a relationship. It could be because they are married and have kids. Also, dealing with an ex who is a narcissist can be quite difficult.

Narcissists are potentially harmful in many ways. How do you simply make the relationship work? How is it possible to build a healthy relationship with a narcissist? It is possible and maybe rewarding to have a relationship with someone who is a narcissist. Still, that relationship could be psychologically and emotionally draining. A narcissist usually lacks what it takes to build a strong relationship. They do not show consistent kindness, compassion, selflessness, reciprocity, compromise, and empathy. They drain the energy and spirit from their supposed partners, turning them into symbolic punching bags.

What to expect in a relationship with a narcissist

Being in a relationship or having any connection with a narcissist has many challenges. Still, when you are aware of what to expect, you should know how to handle the relationship better so you can build a healthy one.

<u>You will need to make some sacrifices</u>

To have a fairly good life or relationship with a narcissist, you need to make many sacrifices to keep the relationship going. You will sacrifice a part of yourself, especially your beliefs and what you stand for. One of the expected constants is that you will be lied to over and over, yet must accept it.

Narcissists are crafty and very manipulative. They are good at changing the narrative and altering reality into the version that suits them. In the end, they get you to agree to something that you didn't do. To keep narcissists happy, you will need to learn how to accept their version of reality as the truth of what has happened even when it is not. That way, you will always escape their fury and not be on the receiving end of their anger.

Part of the sacrifice is that you might never be praised for achieving something or rewarded for behaving well. At every opportunity, a narcissist will try to undermine your efforts. They are manipulative to the point where they call all the shots yet in a very shrewd way that makes it seem as though you are in control. They will let you make some decisions but then do something different, and you have to appreciate them for doing that.

Building healthy relationships with narcissists mean you have to play a secondary role. You need to make sacrifices that will drain you in many ways.

<u>To a narcissist, no one is to be trusted</u>

Narcissists don't trust anybody except themselves. Even when you do everything right and have never given them any reason for not trusting you, they still will not respect you enough to allow you to lead your life without interference and surveillance. They may go to the extent of spying and stalking you.

Narcissists have a habit of tracking their partners. In a romantic relationship, narcissists are likely to install trackers without the knowledge of their partners. It could be on their phone or computer, and they feel no remorse about it. In fact, they are rather proud of their actions.

Regrettably, most narcissists abuse drugs and alcohol to the extreme. Their partners will have to endure the abuse, adapt to their lifestyle, and live with the perpetual fear and expectation that they may take things too far with the drugs or alcohol and act unpredictably.

Most narcissists develop bad habits and, because of this, will become so irresponsible that they begin missing appointments, meetings, and work. Therefore, it puts their partners in situations where they have to clean up the mess they create and makeup excuses to absolve them. The partners have been conditioned to believe that they are a team and that it's them against the whole world.

Narcissists will never put their trust in anyone; therefore, they use words that will keep their victims spellbound, like "You are my world" and "Without you, I'm nothing." That way, their victims are comforted with a false sense of security. Meanwhile, they are just keeping their partners from everyone and everything, pitching them against the world and using them.

Narcissists will say things and take convincing actions to make you believe in them, trust them, and risk it all for them. You should be prepared not to be trusted when in a relationship with a narcissist.

Although it is not clear if narcissists do things intending to hurt their partners to the level they do, they excuse having a bad childhood. You must understand and forgive them for all their shortcomings and behaviors. They will explode, and you will face their rage if you don't forgive them for everything they had done, including the times when they abused you.

<u>You will be drained and tapped out</u>

Narcissists don't like taking the blame for anything. They look for someone else to take the blame, and you who have a relationship with one will likely be the person to fill that role. Therefore, to make your relationship work, you will have to come to terms with the fact that you will be the scapegoat at every opportunity and probably be demeaned. If you don't want to take the blame for them, the narcissistic traits will kick in, and they will accuse you of being crazy and inconsiderate. Mostly, all your feelings will be used against you to make you feel bad.

To make such a relationship work, you should be ready to put your self-interest behind you and be prepared to be harassed because everything that goes wrong is your fault. You will need to lose yourself. The things you love, the things you like, the fun things you do, your music choice, books, and movies will all be termed bad or uncool. To them, you have terrible taste. They will gradually mold you into somebody you are not.

To keep a narcissist happy, you might need to lose your friends, family, and even your job. You might have to stop pursuing your career and interests. You will have to live for them to be happy. Your life will revolve around them to keep the relationship going and keep them happy. You will stay home all day doing chores. Still, all that won't get you any accolades. They will then call you a boring person.

Some narcissists would rather have you keep your job so that you can help keep their lifestyle financed, milking you while you slave for their happiness.

By now, you have most likely determined that you are in a one-way relationship with a very self-centered person. You have, in all probability, learned a good deal about your relationship. Most likely, you are considering making some changes. Are you willing to do things differently in your relationship with your loved one? This chapter will help you explore whether you are ready to make some important changes and will then give you some new strategies for managing the narcissist in your life.

Are changes possible?

Change almost always involves overcoming some of your anxieties and taking risks involving your personal growth. You will need to overcome your anxieties about change before you can begin to do things differently. You may ask yourself, "Are changes possible?" and "Should I make them?" Now is the time to make some important choices. You will need to answer some tough questions.

Can you forgive and move forward?

Forgiveness is the starting point. Most likely, your one-way relationship has hurt you in many ways, and you have needed to forgive your partner, friend, or relative in the past, but you will need to do it again. You cannot harbor resentment and maintain a good relationship. Sooner or later, you will have to forgive the narcissist, and the sooner, the better. Fortunately, we are billionaires in forgiveness; we have an endless supply.

Remember, you do not have to feel forgiving to forgive; it is an act of will, a decision you make, not a feeling. Also, forgiving does not mean foolishly assuming that the narcissist will not do more hurtful things in the future; he probably will, and you should be on the alert so as not to be taken advantage of. It may be helpful to remember that forgiveness is also for you. By letting go, you can begin to heal too.

Are you willing to work on just yourself?

Another prerequisite for change is that you need to accept that you can only change yourself. Can you resist the temptation of trying to change the narcissist? It's easy to fall back into old patterns, especially when success is not immediate. You may find yourself asking, "Why do I have to change when he is the problem? Shouldn't it be fifty-fifty?" Quite frankly, we have never known a relationship to be fifty-fifty.

Besides, making changes is empowering because you are in control. Waiting around for others to change just makes you feel weak and angry. You may think it's unfair that you will have to do all the work now since you're the only one who has worked for this relationship all along—after all, it's one-way! But most likely, you have worked in the wrong areas, especially if you have been trying to change the narcissist.

Can your partner love you as you deserve?

To put it bluntly, would you bet on a horse that has never won a race? If the narcissist in your life has never had a successful reciprocal relationship, you are making this bet. Oh, sure, the narcissist will claim to love you, but there are many types of love. At two years old, a baby loves his mother, but that is not the type of love you look for in a romantic partner or a friend. The narcissist's level of love is immature, but it is all that he knows. Can he grow in his level of maturity in loving? That is a tough one to call. Past success is a good predictor: Have you seen any maturation since you have known him? If so, there is hope.

Are you ready to get the help you need?

You should seriously consider getting professional help in your one-way relationship. We recommend finding an expert who has a history of working with narcissistic clients. Narcissists can be quite challenging for therapists, especially those who are not trained to work with them, so it's important to put some effort into finding someone with the right experience. A good resource might be a local university with a graduate program in clinical psychology, or you can try the Institute for Advanced Studies in Personality and Psychopathology in Port Jervis, New York, or the Personality Disorders Institute at Cornell University.

Both institutes train clinicians to treat narcissistic people and may be able to recommend an expert in your area. (See resources for more information.) When contacting a professional, you will want to make an appointment for yourself; if the narcissist agrees to come, all the better. True friends and trusted family members can also be a good source of emotional support and encouragement, and you'll need them if you decide to make changes.

There is also a good deal of reading material on narcissism, including information on the Internet. You will want to read all you can and become an expert. At the very least, you will know more about the topic than the narcissist in your life.

Eliminate negative thinking in relationships

Your mind is like a garden, and we are the master gardener enthusiasts. We can produce an agricultural masterpiece through care and persistence, but our yard will be a mass of weeds—downsides, instabilities, and failures through neglect. Understanding this, it becomes our duty to remove negative thinking. There are four exceptional techniques for removing the downsides from your mind. Each method is unique and independent from the others. Several of these strategies will undoubtedly seem inconsistent. However, each will definitely be very effective in dealing with negative thinking.

Cut it off.

With this method, the moment you identify that you are assuming a negative idea, you end it. You do not stay with it, and you do not analyze it, you do not shield against it on your own. The moment you realize that you are thinking about an unfavorable idea, just make the right choice in your mind.

Tag it.

As quickly as you acknowledge that you are considering a negative thought, tag it with the first technique rather than cutting it off. Write it down in bold letters and read it at least three times before you continue. You want it to be imprinted into your mind.

Obstacles only have power over you if you respond to them.

Go back and read it again. Continue to read this statement until you realize that reacting to problems is what provides power to them. The minute you begin worrying, start responding to the negative, and take the blame, it has taken over you.

When you acknowledge that the negativity only has power over you when responding to it, you choose not to react. Tag it. Remember that it is only a negative idea and then move on to another thing. Don't get trapped into thinking about it. Disregard it. Once again, they only have power over you if you react to them.

Overemphasize the assumed into all ridiculousness.

The overestimation technique is a fantastic method; however, you must exaggerate it right into ridiculousness. The keyword is ridiculousness. Imagine that you're a salesperson out making your sales calls when the thought comes to you, "Ah, what's the use? I'm not going to make any more sales today."

Afterward, you decide on your own, "Wait for a second... that's an unfavorable thought." With the exaggeration method, what you might say next is, "That's right, I'm not likely to make another sale today."

I won't be shocked if people are ready to throw buckets of water at me as quickly as I open the door. After that, they're most likely to launch pit bull terriers as well as German guards. I'm going to be attacked as well as I'm going to be wet. Then this great big mechanical boxing glove will undoubtedly appear, and it's most likely to smash me in the face.

Wouldn't it be wonderful if, when we have negative thoughts, they include warning signs reading, "It's only an adverse thought; you do not need to believe it if you don't want to." Yet, problems do not come like that. They come camouflaged as genuine issues or silently when we're not paying attention.

If we're not knowledgeable about the fact that our mind is a fantastic impostor, forever invoking unpleasant thoughts, we'll buy into every devastating idea that strikes us. However, with these methods, we have ways of taking care of the negative issues. That's why they are so useful.

Combat the negative with the exact opposite.

Whenever the undesirable is clinging to you, you can neutralize it by believing the exact opposite. When the negative thinking concerns you, "I'm not going to make another sale today," you offset it with, "I'm most likely to make several more sales today." When the adverse idea takes control of you, "I'm never going to get ahead monetarily," you counteract it with the exact reverse, "I'm most likely to be enormously successful monetarily." When the thought comes to you, "I'm never going to have a meaningful relationship," you neutralize it with the opposite, "I'm going to have a fabulous relationship." You see, the mind can think just one thought at a time, so make it positive.

It might seem to you that you're assuming many thoughts at once, yet what is taking place is you're thinking one idea after another, and more. At any given minute, you're only thinking of one idea. So, if you secure the difficult thoughts and also do the exact opposite, you arc taking power away from that unfavorable thought. Don't feed the beast. Frequently, this is contrary to what the majority of people do. When there is something that they don't intend to have happened to them, most individuals think about it, and they focus on it. Eventually, they can materialize it.

Rebuilding a new life

When you're forced to recognize that you have lost the person you assumed was "the one," it resembles starting from scratch. Your life, as you once understood it, disappears, and you find yourself standing there alone, trying to find out what's next. Your self-confidence is shot. The future you had planned on is now gone, and it's hard not to feel confused or too terrified. In addition, there is the pain of such a loss. However, people are resilient; we can get better from this kind of dissatisfaction. We have the capability to turn things around, make favorable adjustments for our future, and rebuild everything that has been shed. Of course, you're doing all that restoring on your own, but after losing "the one," it's better to be alone for a while anyway. Believe me on this one!

Talk it out

I honestly believe that everyone who's rid themselves of a person they thought they'd invest their lives with must enter treatment. Speaking with an expert can seriously help you to grow. If you're brand new to therapy, know that it's experimentation. You may not love the first couple of therapists you meet, so do not settle. You're about to have a very intimate relationship with this person as you "spill the beans" concerning your entire life to them, so you need to find a person who makes you feel comfortable.

If professional treatment isn't for you, talk with another person in your life who is encouraging, whether it is a pal, coworker, family member, etc.

Modify your environment

If you intend to change your life, you will also need to change your things around you. Moving halfway around the world sounds wonderful. Theoretically, it's not the most effective move to make. Instead, make changes to the environment where you already live. For example, I painted my walls, tossed out all my bedding in exchange for new, much more vivid ones, and repositioned my furniture. When you're reconstructing your life, you need to concentrate on yourself, what you desire, and what changes make sense in this new phase.

Look for what interests you

To restructure, you need to put yourself out there. You need to grow, meet new people, sign up for courses, as well as go out to events—generally anything that ignites your interests. You might enroll in some courses that you think are intriguing before finding something that's the right fit. Regardless, you're not just creating the necessary interruption that we all require after losing "the one," but you're concentrating on what benefits this brand-new you.

Have some flings

Although it will take some time to return to dating once again, have a few flings when you are preparing. Don't try to delve into something major, but instead, date several people and enjoy some variety. Date people that aren't your type. Have casual sex with a person you would have never considered having casual sex with before you got rid of "the one." You should think about this part of your life as a transitional period and a necessary one before you agree to fully open your heart once more.

Create a happiness routine

You can't just dream all day. You need to create a regimen that brings you bliss and produces energy and knowledge to trust your own on how to load your cup initially.

Start by making a list of points you delight in doing to take care of your mind and soul. It could be having tea in the morning, taking a walk, or listening to an inspirational podcast. Whatever it is, make a checklist and pick three points you can do every day that will sustain your soul. This goes to developing a routine of caring and will be excellent for you.

CONCLUSION

These are some good tips to follow if you have an anxious attachment style. Also, remember that people don't exist in discrete all/anything categories. Someone may be somewhat Anxious or somewhat Avoidant. If you are both mature enough to know yourself well and notice and care about your style's impact on the other person, things may be able to work out. The goal is for both people to move toward a more secure style of attachment. And by the way, styles do shift over time as a function of relationships.

A troubled, painful relationship will lead a person to become more insecure in their style (either more Anxious or more Avoidant). Learning to interact with each other Securely will produce more security in your relationship, and in time, each of you will develop a more Secure Attachment Style. Securely attached people have three key qualities: They are available, attentive, and responsive. Practicing these qualities and experiencing them from your partner is what helps Security grow.

Watching a relationship that you have invested your emotions, time, and energy into going down the drain can be heartbreaking. Most couples go through ups and downs in the process of trying to get to know each other and trying to build a life together. Understanding what causes these differences and uncovering your hidden insecurities is the most effective way to overcome anxiety and build lasting relationships.

Love is often not enough to sustain a relationship. Trust, intimacy, openness, a willingness to compromise, and secure attachment are also required if a relationship succeeds. Just like it takes two people to make a healthy relationship, it also takes two people to break a relationship.

A willingness to recognize the role we play in our relationships creates the room we need for improvement. When it comes down to building a healthy relationship, there is no room for blaming and scapegoating. Start by accepting that you are equally responsible for what is going on in your relationship. Then start working towards a better future together.

This book aims to equip you with the necessary information and tools to build a healthier relationship. The strategies provided herein are meant to be practical and easy to follow no matter what stage your relationship is in. It could be months, years, or decades old, but the ingredients for a healthy relationship are constant for any of these stages.

The importance of communication, conflict resolution, emotionally focused therapy, and many other pertinent topics relating to relationships have all been covered comprehensively in this book. We hope that your understanding of the dynamics of your relationship is now much better than when you started reading this book.

You have already taken the first step to creating a healthy relationship by reading this book. The next step is to start applying the principles described in this book. Start small and implement changes gradually at a pace that is manageable for you and your partner. Remember, you can adopt the strategies that seem better suited for your relationship and leave the rest for when you need them.

Love does indeed make the world go round, but you need to create a solid enough foundation to support the love in your relationship. Do not leave the fate of your relationship up to destiny. You have been empowered to take charge of your relationship and make it what you want it to be.

It is our sincere hope that this book will help you improve your relationship.

Thank you for reading!

UP

URANUS
PUBLISHING

www.ingramcontent.com/pod-product-compliance
Lightning Source LLC
Chambersburg PA
CBHW050732030426
42336CB00012B/1534